Praise for *Praying Their Way*

"*Praying Their Way* is a true gift—for parents, ministry leaders, and anyone who cares about nurturing children's spiritual lives."

–Johannah Myers, D.Min, Executive Director,
Messy Church USA

"This book is a blessing to any parent, pastor, or youth leader who has ever felt ill-equipped to help a middle schooler spend quality time with God through prayer. It's a joy to read and do, keep and give, visit and revisit."

–Rev. Dr. Ruth L. Boling, PC(USA) pastor and author of
Come Worship With Me and *Season's Greetings*

"*Praying Their Way* is a tender and reflective guide to helping kids encounter God in prayer. This work invites us all to slow down, listen deeply, and remember that friendship with God is for every age."

–Traci Smith, Director of Family Faith Every Day
and author of *Faithful Families*

"Mary Clare Owens and her dad Roger have written such a beautiful and theologically rich resource together, perfect for tweens and the grown-ups in their lives! This book is theology, story, and practice woven together in one handbook perfect for ministry leaders, caregivers, and the students themselves."

–Rev. Melissa Collier Gepford,
Intergenerational Discipleship Coordinator,
Great Plains Conference of The United Methodist Church

"Roger Owens has created something rare and beautiful: a book about prayer that feels less like instruction and more like invitation. What makes this work truly special is the collaboration with Roger's daughter, Mary Clare, whose honest reflections and questions ground the manuscript in the lived experience of a young person discovering God."

– Sophfronia Scott, author of *This Child of Faith*
and *The Seeker and the Monk*

"*Praying Their Way* is a testament to the innate wisdom and spiritual capacity of children. As a mother, a lay pastor, a therapist, and a professor, I can incorporate each of Roger and Mary Clare's prayer practices into my life and work."

–Sarah Flannery, Assistant Professor of Marriage
and Family Therapy, Louisville Seminary

"I have never read a book so appropriately written to 'tweens.' It speaks openly and clearly without a hint of condescension."

– Rev. Dr. Leanne Hadley, Associate Pastor,
First United Methodist Church, Frankfort, Kentucky

"I loved the engaging stories, honest experiences, and 'Ways to Pray' guides. Roger and Mary Clare offer a much-needed book on prayer for tweens and adults alike."

–Rev. Kathy Pittenger, deacon in the Michigan Conference
of The United Methodist Church

praying their way

24 PRAYER PRACTICES FOR KIDS AND THE ADULTS WHO LOVE THEM

L. ROGER OWENS WITH MARY CLARE OWENS

UPPER ROOM BOOKS®
NASHVILLE

PRAYING THEIR WAY: 24 Prayer Practices for Kids and the Adults Who Love Them

ISBN: 978-0-8358-2063-9

Epub ISBN: 978-0-8358-2064-6

Cover design: Emily Weigel

Interior design: PerfecType, Nashville, TN

Printed in the United States of America

For more information on resources available from The Upper Room

call 1-800-972-0433 or visit www.upperroom.org

For

Ginger, aka, Mom

with much love, Roger and Mary Clare

contents

introduction

Friendship with God

The scene where Jesus blesses the children is, to me, one of the most touching in the whole New Testament. The disciples were blocking the people from bringing their children to Jesus, and their behavior angered him. "Let the children come to me," Jesus said. "Do not stop them" (Mark 10:14).

I don't know exactly what the scene looked like after Jesus spoke those words. Mark tells us that he took the children in his arms and blessed them. Maybe it ended there, or maybe the moment continued for a while longer. Personally, I hope it looked like the children's message time at a church where I was once a member.

About a third of the way into our strait-laced worship service, Rick, the children's minister, would shout, "Come on down!" like he was hosting *The Price Is Right*. And that's exactly what the children would do—they'd slide out of their pews and scurry to the front of the sanctuary. Some would race, leaving us, the dignified adults, to worry that they'd trip. Others would saunter, knowing from experience that Rick wouldn't begin until they reached him.

One boy often jabbered loudly all the way down the aisle, usually about something related to computer science, but I was never completely sure. He was our resident skeptic, but he never stayed in his pew when the kids were invited to come forward. It was a joyous, raucous occasion—one that I'm certain prompted at least a few worshipers to wonder, *Do they have to run in the sanctuary?* Most of the others, I suspect, wished they still had the energy and youthful spirit of these kids.

When we look back at this story from Mark, Jesus's point is clear: The blessing of relationship with God is not restricted to the folks who have been tested and approved. The beauty of living a life with God is not reserved for those who have learned how to sit still and worship in an orderly, well-mannered way. The joy of divine love is not solely for those who intellectually grasp what faith is all about. Who could claim such understanding anyway? Life with God isn't like an amusement park ride. There are no operators measuring you to make sure you're tall enough to board. No one is checking credentials to see if you're worthy of being loved.

Prayer names the way we enter into a relationship with God. Therefore, prayer itself—that mystery of communication and communion with our Creator—belongs to children as well. Perhaps, if Jesus is to be believed, it belongs to them most of all. Prayer is a primary way children can come to him.

But there's also a problem. When we think about the kids running up for the children's message, full of enthusiasm and joy, we know that they are primarily excited for a time of childish antics and kid-friendly silliness. They are open to praying because it feels like playing. They are willing to wave their hands and jump around. They don't really care how they look in front of a hundred adult worshipers.

These same kids attend Vacation Bible School every summer. They relish learning the motions to songs, doing crafts, and playing whatever games adults have concocted for them. They do their best to sit through the Bible lessons. These little ones are easy to reach, to talk to about prayer.

But their older siblings, their middle-grade brothers and sisters (roughly grades 5-8), stay behind in the pews during the children's message and eventually age out of VBS. They are too old for the silliness that makes up the toolkit of every children's minister, but still too young to roll their eyes like jaded high schoolers. There is a gap here. Not only are there few resources aimed at helping adults reach older kids to invite them to a life of prayer, there is also a lack of attention paid to the problem. What should we do about these kids, aptly named "tweens"? How can we reach these kids lodged between the other two well-defined age groups?

This book aims to help address that gap.

Like all of us when it comes to prayer, these kids need people to guide them—parents, grandparents, godparents, pastors, children's ministers, and Sunday school teachers. They need grown-ups who will engage them in the practice of prayer, mentors who will help them tap into their natural curiosity about God, a curiosity they haven't yet outgrown, and allow them to embrace their innate draw toward mystery. They need a comforting presence to lead them to the God of Jesus, who stands with arms wide open—a God who wants to bless them and be their friend.

Children of this age are the perfect age to become friends with the God who longs to befriend them. Because every age is the perfect age for *that*.

If you are holding this book, then there's a simple truth that I can guess about you: You are one of those people called to the holy—and fun—task of welcoming kids like this into a life of prayer.

Father and Daughter Learn to Pray

As a father, I have always wanted to be one of those people.

I grew up in a family that was close-lipped about the life of faith. We had a green bonded-leather Bible that sat on the coffee table, a brass bookmark protruding from the top edge. That Bible got dusted weekly, but I don't remember ever seeing the bookmark move to a different place. If my parents prayed—and, for all I know, they did—they never talked to me about it. Neither do I remember my Sunday school teachers—wonderful in every way, especially because they brought us donuts most Sundays—talking about prayer or how to approach Jesus as a friend, as he himself invites kids to do.

As a result, when my boys were young, I didn't know how to talk to them about prayer. Even though I was a pastor with a PhD in theology, that Midwestern reserve that I'd internalized from my childhood got in the way. I knew how to do a lot of other things—I taught them to shoot a basket, bait a hook, rinse their plates after dinner (though that still hasn't caught on). I played with them, wrestled with them, and sang with them. But I felt unsure about how to let down the drawbridge for them and open the interior castle of my heart. I was still learning how to live with God myself, never mind trying to teach someone else.

By the time the boys were in high school, Mary Clare, my daughter, was a middle-grader. I would put her to bed every night, and we began to have meaningful conversations about deeper things, initiated mostly by her own interest. She wondered aloud about God. She pondered the topic of death. She wanted to understand the loneliness and fear that sometimes descends in the late-night hours. And she asked about prayer. In most of our chats, I let her curiosity guide the conversation, trying to avoid letting any of my "answers" squash her own searching.

During these bedtime routines, we'd laugh and play with her stuffed animals (the best nights were when her stuffed animals would host a talent competition). As the bedtime antics downshifted into the quiet minutes before sleep, we'd discuss the mysteries of life, which would eventually lead to prayer. I'd always end our time together by singing a song based on a famous prayer of St. Teresa of Avila that affirms that when we are afraid, God is enough.[1] Then I'd kiss Mary Clare goodnight, turn out the light, and leave her to sleep in God's care.

It was fortuitous that her growing curiosity met my own emerging confidence when talking about that beautiful, mysterious, and sometimes confounding relationship with God called prayer.

When she was twelve, Mary Clare received a book for kids on mindfulness and meditation as a gift. It was lavishly illustrated and filled with easy-to-follow guidelines for a variety of different meditations. Not a religious book, it was aimed at fostering attention, calmness, and resilience in kids. Sometimes she would ask me to lead her through one of the meditations before bed. I appreciated how easily the book equipped me to do this. Mary Clare enjoyed these experiences so much that she began writing her own meditations. One evening before bed, she showed me a meditation she'd written and asked if *she* could lead *me* through it. This time I was the one lying on the bed, sinking into calm, and Mary Clare was my guide.

During these moments I began to wonder: Where is the book about prayer that does what this book has done with meditation? Where is the resource that equips adults to lead these older kids through the experience of joy and peace that comes from living an authentic Christian spiritual life? Where is the book that helps kids root their lives in prayerful communion with God?

By this point in my life, I'd been a professor of Christian spirituality for years, introducing practices of prayer to people preparing for ministry and instructing them on how to lead others in prayer. I'd studied and taught the Christian spiritual traditions in both classrooms and churches, and I'd written books on spirituality for adults. Now my nightly routines with my daughter were showing me how meaningful those same Christian spiritual traditions could be for kids when they are offered in a safe environment that honors a kid's own curiosity, questions, and longing.

Kids have spiritual lives that are already deeply attuned to God, so I wanted to write a resource that would empower adults to help kids open the door to prayer, a door that they are already naturally poised to walk through. This is the book I wish the grown-ups in my life had when I was a kid. This is the book I wish *I* had when my boys were younger. This is the book I've been blessed to write, inspired by my own daughter's desire for God.

Obstacles

I don't think any of us want to intentionally stand in the way of kids reaching Jesus like the disciples did in Mark 10. We don't want to be the ones preventing children from encountering God. But my own experience tells me there are obstacles standing in the way of leading the kids in our lives to experience the joy and mystery of prayer.

One obstacle is simply that prayer feels so private. We don't always know how to talk about it. We might not even have any experience talking about it. When teaching his disciples about prayer, Jesus told them to go into a room, shut the door, and spend time with God in secret. When he prayed himself, Jesus often rose early in the morning and sought out a deserted place so he could be alone with the one he called Abba. Jesus's example shows us that prayer is the most intimate part of our relationship with God. How, we wonder, can we talk about that relationship with others, especially children? How can we invite them into that sacred place of communion and trust, when it so often feels like a padlocked room within our own hearts?

While it's true that prayer is deeply personal, it's not intended to be private. It's meant to be shared. In John 17, Jesus prays to God at length, and he does so quite publicly. As part of his prayer, he asks God to protect his followers and help them remain united, enjoying a life together with God. Earlier, when his disciples asked him to teach them to pray, he offered them the model prayer that we have come to call the Lord's Prayer, a prayer that begins with the first-person plural: "*Our* Father in heaven" (Matt. 6:9). The very fact that Jesus's disciples asked him to teach them to pray is an indication that prayer can be learned and shared with others despite gesturing to something deeply personal.

Perhaps the biggest clue that prayer shouldn't remain private—and that it's something we *should* invite the kids we love to participate in—is our own longing: the way we long for the kids in our lives, whether children, grandchildren, or the young ones in our congregations, to taste the joy, hope, and confidence that comes from growing in friendship with God, a relationship that is sustained through prayer.

However much we may want to help kids discover a life of prayer, a second obstacle stymies us: Many adults lack the confidence in their own spiritual lives to teach kids about theirs. We can teach them specific prayers, of course, like the simple table grace my family started saying when our kids were small and continue to use to this day: "Dear Jesus, thank you for loving us. Thank you for this food and blessings. Amen." That's a breeze.

But few of us (even many of us who have been to seminary!) feel equipped to introduce kids to practices like praying with Scripture, communing with God in silence, or encountering God through creation. We might feel like we are not good enough at praying to teach anyone at all. We may be unsatisfied that our own prayers don't feel the way we think they should, or we may fret that we don't pray as regularly as we ought. We taste few moments of prayerful ecstasy, we live distracted lives, and we rarely hear from God. Who are we, we might think, to teach kids to pray?

This book aims to address these doubts and obstacles. For those who need to escape the prison of privacy when it comes to prayer, this book provides models for talking about prayer and includes prompts to start conversations that alleviate the anxiety that comes with broaching the subject of prayer, especially with kids.

More importantly, this book provides accessible guides for leading kids through a wide variety of prayer practices. The simple fact is that there are no experts in prayer. We are, all of us, always beginners. I hope that everyone who wants to welcome kids onto the ride that is a life with God will find the prayer guides in this book easy to use. No seminary degree or certificate in children's ministry is required.

I hope that as you use this book to introduce kids to prayer and as you lead them in practices of prayer, your own confidence will grow. I hope that along the way you begin to discover the kind of life in God's love for which you've been longing. I can't think of anything more beautiful than this: Grown-ups and kids together, riding alongside each other in a joyful life with God.

About this Book

This book is a guide written to help you feel more confident and better equipped as you lead kids to explore a life of prayer.

This book is divided into two parts: a conversation about what prayer means and a guide for different ways to pray.

Since most of us have limited experience thinking about what prayer is, let alone talking about it, this book contains twelve short chapters to start conversations about prayer. With titles like "No Right Way," "Friendship with God," and "Prayer is Natural," each short chapter addresses an aspect of prayer I have come to believe is crucial for us to feel free and uninhibited in our life of prayer.

In short, these chapters address a handful of topics that are important for kids to encounter when talking about prayer. I've written these chapters as if I'm addressing the kids themselves. I've imagined myself in front of a room full of twelve-year olds and written directly to them. I've done this to offer a model based on how I've learned to talk about prayer with my own daughter.

Each of these chapters concludes with "Conversation Starters" to ease your way into a dialogue with kids around the ideas conveyed. You can choose to summarize these topics for kids in your own words, read sections of these chapters aloud to them, or, for older kids, encourage them to read the chapters for themselves. They should be a fun read for adults and kids, as they seek to inject some lightness into what can feel like a serious topic.

While conversation about prayer is critical, it's no substitute for the experience of prayer itself. And there are myriad ways to pray, more than many of us have been led to believe. Kids will flourish in prayer when they have adults who can show them the fullness and variety of prayer beyond the narrow experiences that most of us have had. This book offers twenty-four different prayer practices for kids, divided into six categories:

- Ways to pray with *scripture*
- Ways to pray that are *quiet*
- Ways to pray with your *body*
- Ways to pray in *nature*
- Ways to pray *together*
- Ways to pray for *justice*

Each prayer practice begins with a brief introduction written specifically for adults. This introduction contains some background to help you understand how each practice is prayer and includes suggestions for how to use it with kids.

The prayer guides themselves are written in the second person and are addressed directly to kids. This means that you can use each prayer guide as a kind of script as you guide kids through the practice the first few times until the kids feel ready to engage the practice on their own.

What I've enjoyed most about writing this book is that Mary Clare has joined me as a collaborator (she was thirteen when we started the book, fifteen when we finished). You'll see throughout the book that there are brief reflections written by Mary Clare on her experiences with some of the prayer practices, as well as her thoughts on several of the short chapters. Our nightly routines have turned into a shared project, as Mary Clare has read and given me feedback on each part of this book, "test-driving" much of it, so to speak, to assure that this book is accessible to the middle-grade kids to whom it is aimed.

While this book will be useful to younger kids as well, you will need to do more to adapt it for them. Read through the chapters and decide which ideas seem the most important for you to share with the younger elementary-aged kids you are working with, and feel free to modify the practices in any way that seems helpful for kids in first through fourth grades.

Older kids, in the fifth- through eighth-grade range, should be able to benefit from the book as it is written, and some will even find pleasure in reading the chapters and working through the prayer guides themselves. Kids in the seventh grade and beyond should have no problem picking up this book on their own, but don't miss out on the opportunity—and joy—of sharing a spiritual journey with them as well.

However old the kids you are working with, I want to make one suggestion: Use this book alongside others. Kids and grown-ups can work through it together. A group of middle schoolers can meet every other week at someone's house, led by an adult, to talk about how using these practices is going. Children's ministers and children's ministry volunteers can use this book to help equip a group of adults to lead their kids at home (and grow in their own spiritual lives as well). Middle school youth leaders can use the book to shape youth group meetings. Prayer can become something we share, something we talk about, and something that feels familiar and no longer foreign.

The more we invite each other into practices of prayer and conversation about a life of friendship with God, the more comfortable prayer will become. Not only that, but it will also be more fun. Because almost everything is more fun when done with others, right?

Mary Clare and I are grateful that you are using this book. We are praying for both you and the kids who are a part of your life. When you use this book with kids, we pray that . . .

They will find joy in relationship with God.
They will stay curious when prayer feels boring.
They will persevere when prayer gets challenging.
They will laugh when it seems the right thing to do.
They will ask questions when they are confused.

On occasion, when they pray, they will feel surrounded by the sweet, sweet, oh-so-sweet love of God.

When they don't, they won't worry about it because prayer is a mystery.
Their growing friendship with God will fill their lives with meaning and hope.
They will find others to share this journey of prayer with.
They will hear Jesus's invitation, "Come to me," and nothing will stand in the way.

part one

On Prayer

chapter one

Friendship with God

We are used to thinking about prayer as a time when we simply ask God for things. It is that sometimes, of course, but not all the time. In the Gospel of John, Jesus provides us with a picture that can help us think about prayer a little differently.

After the last meal that Jesus shared with his disciples before he was crucified, Jesus took a towel, knelt down, and washed his disciples' feet. Think of all those feet, covered in dirt and sores—and he got down on the floor and scrubbed them clean, right there after dinner! After washing the feet of the disciples, he said something to them, something important. It might have taken him some time to say this, because I imagine he looked each one of them in the eye as he spoke: "I do not call you servants any longer . . . but I have called you friends" (John 15:15).

Jesus—God in the flesh!—wanted to be their friend.

Not only that, he wants to be your friend too.

Jesus, who is God's love in the flesh, set loose in this world, wants to be our friend.

Think about one of the friends that you have, maybe your best friend. If this friend is a *good* friend, you would probably say that you can trust them, right? Beyond that, you enjoy spending time with your friend; in fact, there's a good chance that you like nothing *more* than spending time with your friend! You'd also likely agree that you can ask your friend for help.

I see Mary Clare and her friends helping each other out all the time—with homework, with picking out clothes, and with giving advice on sensitive topics that they aren't ready to talk to their parents about. Sometimes a friend will help you by just being there. They'll hang out with you while you clean your room or choose a birthday present for your dad or do some other random thing. Asking for and receiving help is such an important part of friendship.

Here's something I also bet you already know: Friendships are *so. much. more.* than simply doing things for each other.

Imagine you need to buy a present for your dad, so you and your friend decide to go to the mall. Maybe the friend will help you find that perfect gift for your dad (as a dad myself, I suggest a box of really good dark chocolate and a gift card to a bookstore), but a lot more than shopping happens when you're there with your friend. You also talk to each other about what's going on in your lives. As you meander from store to store, you complain about the bad grade that Mrs. Shuttleworth gave you on your last test and how unfair it is (she, of course, would call it the grade you *earned*). You might try to make each other laugh so loud that someone gives you a side-eye or try on sneakers that you definitely can't afford, giggling at the ones that are super out of style. You might simply stroll along in silence, glad that your friend is by your side. They didn't have to come to the mall—it's not *their* dad's birthday, after all. But they wanted to be with you.

Because your friendship is all about the *relationship*.

Since God wants to be your friend and Jesus has made it possible for us to be friends with God, then prayer is the way to support and grow that relationship. Sometimes that *does* mean asking for things and seeking help. But other times it means listening. Sometimes prayer is about sharing what's on your heart—your joys, your fears, your feelings of boredom. Other times it's about hanging out with God in silence. In the beginning of the relationship, when things are just getting started and you're getting to know each other, it can be awkward and confusing, like making new friends at school. That's all part of it.

And as with our human friends, it's totally worth it.

There are two other truths about friendship that help us understand prayer.

First, we know that friendships change and grow over time. A relationship doesn't stay the same forever. As you get to know God better—as you get older and more mature—your relationship with God will grow and change. That's natural, and it's also necessary. Imagine some of the silly things you and your friends do now and think about some of the things you talk about. Were you doing those same things two years ago? Were you talking about the same things? Do you think you'll be doing and talking about the same things in thirty years? I strongly doubt it.

In the same way, expect your relationship with God to grow and change. This means that how you pray will change as well.

There's one last thing we should remember. No matter how well you know them, or how many hours you spend together every day, your friend will always remain a mystery to you. You might *think* you know everything about them, but if you stay friends for another fifty years, you'll eventually realize that there's never a way to know everything about someone. In fact, we can't ever really know everything about ourselves. After living for fifty years, I am still a mystery to myself.

As much as you think you know someone—everything they love or hate, their favorite color, their favorite food, their favorite football team, their favorite hangout spot—you can't know *everything*. Each person is a mystery, and you can spend a lifetime getting to know someone.

Now, if a person is a mystery, then how much more of a mystery is God? For all the things that prayer will do, it will not help you "figure God out." You'll never be able to put God in a box, attach a label to it, and say, "There, I've got this sorted. What's next?" The truth is that many people have dedicated their lives to prayer only to discover that God seems *more* mysterious the longer you're in a relationship with God.

God's love will always be bigger and more mysterious than any of us can possibly imagine. But over time, you *can* come to know and trust this love more and more, you *can* know that God's love is there for you through it all, and you *can* know that God will stay close to you—closer than a best friend. God, your friend, will be with you, rejoicing with you in the good times, comforting you in the hard times, and sustaining you in all the times between.

When you say, "I want to learn to pray," you are also saying, "I want to grow in friendship with God. I want to know the mysterious love that created me and sustains me, the love that longs more than anything to be with me in this life." It is a good thing to want that, and I want it for you too.

Mary Clare says . . .

I will never forget meeting one of my best friends in kindergarten. I remember sitting on a little square carpet, happily building with wooden blocks, until a blonde girl came up to me and asked, in a voice that was almost a whisper, "Can I play with you?" Of course, I was happy to have a play partner, so I replied, "Sure!" But instead of jumping right in and helping me make a tower for a princess or a bridge over imaginary water, she wordlessly sat next to me and watched as I continued to play.

That was the first time we ever hung out together but certainly was not the last. As we became closer friends and her shyness faded, we would search for fairies in her backyard, compare and trade trinkets we found lying around the elementary school, or race to get seats together in the cafeteria. We spent loads of time together, but as we grew and changed, so did our friendship.

As we've matured, we've become more open with each other. Being one of my best friends, I can trust her to talk with about many things—crushes I have, people who have made me feel sad or angry, or deep thoughts I'm having at night—and she can talk to me about the same. We both know that we have each other's full support when there's good news or a shoulder to cry on when there isn't.

As I meet new people, I keep in mind that relationships form and change with time. Making friends now may not be as easy as it was in kindergarten, but the time spent with them and the trust gained is worth it in the long run. I think of this with prayer as well. A relationship with God takes time, but I know through my relationship with God that God is trustworthy, supportive, and loves me for who I am. It is so comforting to know that God is here for me now and that God will be there for me in all my years to come, even if that's in a different way than before.

conversation starters

- Have a conversation about a friendship that has grown and changed over time. What was it like when the friendship first started? What is it like now?
- Do you find the idea of friendship with God helpful, comforting, or, possibly, confusing? How can the idea of God as our friend help us understand what it's like to have a relationship with God?
- What are some steps you might take to help God know that you want this friendship too?

chapter two

God Is Here

Once, there was a little fish swimming in the ocean. He swam up to an older, wiser fish and asked, "Can you help me, please? I'm looking for this thing called 'the ocean.' Can you help me find it?" The older, wiser fish looked puzzled and said, "This *is* the ocean—it's all around you." The little fish looked disappointed and responded, "No, this is just water. I'm looking for the *ocean*." And he swam away, sad.[2]

Don't you just want to yell to the little fish, "Look around, little fish! The ocean is all around you!"

Some of us have been taught to believe that there is a distance between us and God, that somehow there is a gap between us that needs to be bridged. Sometimes we *feel* that God is far away or even absent. We get the sense that God has gone on a long vacation—maybe to Italy, Rome seems nice—and hasn't announced a return date. We might not be able to explain it, but it's undeniable: It can feel like God is somewhere *else*.

Trust me, I know the feeling.

But even though you may have been taught that we are separate from God and that our problem, as human beings, is that we have to find God and construct a bridge to cross the canyon between God and us, that doesn't mean it's true. And even if we *feel* like God is absent—maybe hanging out on a boat off the coast of Italy with no cell service—that doesn't mean it's true either.

What we've been taught doesn't determine where God is. Neither do our feelings.

The truth is, God is closer than you think, because God is right here. God is all around us and within us.

I'm going to say something that might sound confusing. It's something a Christian thinker said about 1,600 years ago. I'm also not going to explain it. I'm just going to place it right here—like a lovely piece of art hanging on the wall—for you to think about or talk about with a friend or a grown-up so you can try to make some sense out of it. I'm sharing this because I believe that it's true.

Here's what that ancient Christian said:

"God is closer to me than I am to myself."[3]

And God is closer to *you* than you are too yourself too.

Paul, one of the earliest Christians and the man who wrote many of the letters that make up the New Testament, had a passion: He wanted to let all people know about Jesus's love and forgiveness, because there were many people who had never heard of Jesus. He wanted the people to know that God desires to be everybody's friend through Jesus, even people who hadn't heard of Jesus.

Once, he went to Athens in Greece carrying this same message (Acts 17:16-34). This was a long time ago, when people in Greece worshiped a bunch of different gods (you've probably studied the stories of the Greek gods and goddesses on Mt. Olympus in school or read about them in books about a kid named Percy Jackson). The whole city was full of statues dedicated to these gods.

When Paul arrived, he noticed that there was one altar marked with the dedication, "To an Unknown God." You see, the people were covering their bases just in case there was another god out there that they'd never heard of. Paul said to them something like, *You worship this unknown God, but let me tell you something: I know who this God is! This is the God who made all things—the one and only true God. You've been searching for God, but you need to know that all those other gods and their statues are fake—you made them with your own hands. You've been searching, and I can declare to you: The God you are searching for is closer than you think.* Then he said, in language that might sound a little strange, that God is the one in whom "we live and move and have our being" (Acts 17:28).

That's an odd way to put that, isn't it? *In God we live and move and have our being.*

But I think that's Paul's way of saying that we are like the little fish and God is the ocean. God is all around us. And in us. And close to us. So close to us. But we don't always realize it, or we don't care, or maybe we simply don't take the time to notice. Paul was telling the people of Athens, in so many words, "Wake up! Look around! God is here!" Martin Laird, one of my favorite writers about topics like God and prayer, once wrote, "God does not know how to be absent."[4]

That's not the same for us. You know how to be absent. If you wake up sick one morning, then a grown-up emails your teachers to tell them that you're ill. The next day, or whenever you go back to school, you ask a friend to tell you what you missed.

A teacher knows how to be absent too. They call the principal of the school, and the principal gets a substitute teacher for the day. If you get lucky, then it's the silly one who lets you goof off or watch movies.

Parents know how to be absent. They have long days at work and might have to make a sad phone call or send a disappointing text to say that their job, or some other responsibility, will be keeping them from going to see your soccer match or might make them miss dinner that night.

Everybody we know or have ever met knows how to be absent. As humans, we can only be in one place at a time. If we are *here* (wherever *here* happens to be at the moment), then we can't be *there.*

But that's not the same for God. God is the ocean. Can the ocean ever be far away from the fish? Can the fish live beyond the ocean? Can they hide from the ocean?

No. Not at all.

God is closer to you than you think because God is always present.

And that's really good news, because God is also love. You are, all the time, with every breath you take and every move you make, surrounded by love. When you are happy and when you are sad, when you are with others and when you are alone, when you are calm and when you are scared, when you are arguing with a sibling and when you are texting a friend, God is there. And that means that love is there too. You are embraced by love. You are swimming in God's love. Always.

Now, just like the fish isn't always thinking about the ocean, we are not always thinking about God or paying attention to God. Also, God is mysterious, so we don't necessarily *feel* God's presence all the time.

But when you decide to take time to pray, whether you're doing so formally or having a casual chat with God before bedtime or crying out to God when you are scared, remember: You don't have to convince God to come close to you and don't need to build a bridge to God. God is already there. Prayer is not like trying to cross a river to get to God on the other side. God is on your side. God is *at* your side. Prayer is more like opening your eyes and your mind and your heart to God, who is already here.

Sometimes when I sit down to pray, I say, "Well God, here I am. And here you are. How lucky for us both."

Mary Clare says . . .

When I was in seventh grade, one of my best friends was preparing for her bat mitzvah. A bat mitzvah is a Jewish ceremony for a girl who is coming of age and transitioning into adulthood. It was a huge deal for her, and it was a huge deal for me to be able to go and support her in this big moment. I was so excited. My mom and I shopped for the perfect dress, my friend practiced her Hebrew chants in front of me to prepare, and her mom even asked me to give a speech at the party following the service. I was stoked to be able to talk about how proud I was of her and to watch her as she became an adult.

The week of the bat mitzvah, though, I got sick. I had caught a lot of colds that year and usually this also meant I would develop a fever. Sure enough, the night before the bat mitzvah, my temperature rose above one hundred and did not go down the next day.

I missed the service. I couldn't make it to the party after, either.

It was so upsetting to me, and to her, but she understood. I couldn't believe that I was missing one of the biggest days of her life. To this day, I am disappointed that I missed it. I sat in my bed with a box of tissues and some hot tea while I watched a livestream of the service and texted her how proud I was. But it never made up for not being able to be there in person.

We're all human, we all get sick, we all miss things. I was absent, but God wasn't and never is. I believe God was with me that day as I cried about missing the service. God was with me as I watched online, and God was with me both during the week leading up to the bat mitzvah and during the week after. And God was with my friend as she took pictures, recited her chanting that she had been so nervous about, and celebrated her achievements that marked adulthood.

It sucks that I couldn't make it, but I know that God could and always can. If you ever miss important things, remind yourself that it's okay. Sometimes it's hard to control your circumstances, but God will never miss important days. God will never miss dull days. God is always there.

conversation starters

- Has it ever seemed to you like God is absent or far away? Talk about a time it seemed like this was true. Why did it feel that way?
- Does it make a difference to you to be reminded that God is close to you all the time, like an ocean of love surrounding you? Why does it matter to know that?
- Talk about ways you can remind yourself of how close God is, especially when God doesn't feel close.

chapter three
God Is Smiling at You

It was early on a Wednesday morning when I walked into the giant room of a local ministry center to guide a few men in the practice of prayer. The men, four of them, sat around a table, styrofoam cups of coffee sitting in front of them, ready for me to take the lead.

One man, named Tom, I knew fairly well. We'd attended the same church for a few years. Tom was gruff, wore a shaggy beard, and I'd never seen him in anything but jeans and a t-shirt. He also made the best macaroni and cheese you've ever had. At every church potluck, the first thing I would do was survey the food to see if Tom had brought his mac and cheese. And I'd do a little hop and a skip if he had. (Seriously, it was really good!)

I opened our time together by asking these men to imagine God smiling at them so that they would feel a sense of welcome as they began to pray. Then, I read a story from the Gospel of Mark where the disciples are in a boat, Jesus is asleep, and a great storm arises while they're out in the middle of the sea. The disciples are so scared that they wake Jesus up. Jesus, in response, calms the storm (Mark 4:35-41).

I told the men to imagine that they were in the boat. I asked them, "What do you see? What do you hear? How do you feel?" After they'd spent time picturing themselves in the story and thinking about these questions, I suggested that they have a quiet conversation with Jesus about what they'd noticed. I told them, "Talk to Jesus about how this story relates to your own life. Maybe your life feels like a boat that's being swamped by waves, and you are longing for Jesus to calm them."

When the time of prayer was over, I asked the men to share a little about any of the challenges they'd experienced while praying. I expected them to say that they struggled to picture the scene, or perhaps that they got distracted and started thinking about other things (like whether there would still be coffee left when we were done or why I hadn't brought donuts). But that wasn't what happened.

Tom was the first to speak, and I'll never forget what he said: "I struggled to imagine God smiling at me. I feel like I'm such a disappointment to God, it's hard for me to think that God would ever smile at me."

My heart broke when he said that. It broke for Tom and for all the other people who carry the weight of feeling like they are a disappointment to God. It broke for all who feel like God would have no good reason to smile at them.

I know that there are lots of people who feel this way, even kids.

We mess up a lot. I know I do. It happens, even when we try our best not to. We get mad and we say things we shouldn't, sometimes to the people closest to us, the people we love the most. We get in a fight with our friends, or we find ourselves telling a lie. We do things we shouldn't do. It's not like we don't know how we should behave, but we often simply don't act the way we know is right.

But there are other times when it's not really under our control. There are those times when we miss a big shot in a basketball game, and we can feel the disapproval coming from our teammates. Or there are the times we bring home a test from school, and a parent says, "If you got a B+, how much harder would you have had to work to get an A-?" These are the moments that make us feel bad. Maybe a group of friends, for reasons we don't fully understand, just abandons us—ejecting us from the group text and not inviting us over to hang out anymore. In these moments, we start to wonder why we are not good enough for them.

So sometimes we *actually* do things we shouldn't, and other times we're made to *think* we've done something wrong. On top of that, some of us have been taught that God is like a mean principal or a difficult grader, more difficult than the harshest teacher we've ever had. With everything we know about ourselves and the way we might see others treating us, we look at God and think, "Wow, God's probably giving us a C+, if we're lucky." We feel like we're barely keeping our head above water in this class called life.

I think that's what my friend Tom felt when he struggled to imagine that God could smile at him. I know Tom is not the only one. There are so many reasons we might feel that way. But you should know: It's not true.

Let me tell you about another friend of mine. Her name is Julian. She lived a little more than six hundred years ago. We've obviously never had dinner or hung out, but she wrote a book that I've read many, many times, and reading that book makes me feel like we're friends.

Julian lived in England, in the city of Norwich, during the fourteenth century. To put it simply, that was a very tough time to be alive. There were diseases going around that killed lots of people, and there wasn't much, if any, medicine to speak of. There were also constant battles and wars about who should be in charge, and people were persecuted and sometimes killed for their religious beliefs. There were lots of people who observed all this death and destruction and said, "Well, God must be pretty upset, I guess this is God punishing us. God is up there with a huge frown on his face!"

Amid these swirling challenges, Julian prayed to know God better. She wanted to understand why there was so much suffering. Now, she never got a clear answer—it turns out, suffering is a mystery—but God did give her a vision, which she wrote about in her book. In the vision one truth became incredibly clear. She heard God say, in so many words, "I am not angry with you."[5]

This puzzled her. She'd been taught that God was angry, and punished people as a result. But here was God affirming the very opposite: *God is not angry with you.*

In other words, yes, we do mess things up sometimes. And, yes, other people sometimes make us feel bad about ourselves even when we *haven't* messed things up. Yes, there are times when we can feel like God wouldn't want to smile on us, that God must be so disappointed, even angry, with us. But that's just not the case.

Over six hundred years ago, Julian heard God say something that I want to make sure you hear today: All of that is bunk. God is *not* angry with you. It's something I try to remember every day.

God loves you. God is smiling on you.

As you work through this book, you'll discover that each of the prayer practices asks you to begin by imagining that God is smiling at you. Prayer starts with feeling welcomed into God's presence and sensing the warmth of God's love. Prayer starts by knowing that, even when we've messed up and other people are angry with us—because other people *do* get angry with us, just as we get angry with other people—nothing can wipe the smile off God's face. Nothing can erase how much God cherishes us.

Nothing at all.

Wherever you go to pray—whether you are walking, riding in a car, struggling to stay awake in church, or sitting in a chair in a basement like I am as I write this—remember this: God is smiling at you. God is glad that you are there, glad that you are *you*. And there is so much delight on God's face—so, so much.

Mary Clare says . . .

At my elementary school, we were given the option to join the orchestra in third grade. Since I've always loved music and had an older brother who played the violin at the time, I jumped at the opportunity to learn violin as well. But things didn't turn out the way I was expecting.

Instead of being taught by Mr. S, the young orchestra teacher known for being incredibly kind and funny, I was going to be taught by an old woman I had never heard of before. She was the exact opposite of Mr. S; she was strict and mean. To my dismay, I realized I wasn't very good at playing the violin. My fingers would get caught up trying to do the correct fingerings on the strings, I couldn't hold the bow the correct way, and I never wanted to practice, because frankly, playing the violin was not fun. There was also an added problem: My teacher would give us paper practice cards every week to record how much we'd practiced each day. And I never did.

The first time a few of us in class came back with blank cards, she scolded us saying, "Hang your heads in shame!" And we literally had to stand in front of the room and droop our heads, reflecting on our shameful lack of practice. It was humiliating.

I switched to band in fourth grade, in part because I decided I was going to be a renowned clarinetist when I grew up, but also because of the hurtful ways my orchestra teacher talked to us.

At one point or another, we all make mistakes. We all say we're going to do something and don't; we all feel as though someone is disappointed in us. That's called being human. Although there are people in life who get angry at us or even try to make us feel shame and guilt for the mistakes we make, God would never tell us to hang our heads in shame. If I could go back, I would tell my third-grade self that God would smile at me for trying something new, and that God would tell me to hold my head up high. And God is saying the same thing to you. God is always smiling at you.

conversation starters

- Have you ever felt that someone was disappointed in you? What was that like?
- Have you ever worried that God is disappointed in you or angry with you? How does that worry make you feel?
- What difference would it make to remember that God is *not* angry with you, but is smiling at you—always?

chapter four

Big Feelings

Were you ever afraid of the dark? Not now, but when you were younger. Were you afraid that monsters were lurking under your bed or hiding in your closet? What did you think they were doing? Were they waiting, biding their time, until your someone tucked you in, kissed you goodnight, and turned out the light so that they could burst out and gobble you up?

Of course, we all know that there aren't actually any monsters under our beds. There are no monsters hiding in the closet. But sometimes it feels like monsters do exist, and they may even exist inside of us.

I remember one of the first times I got very angry, and let me tell you, that *felt* like a monster. It felt like something had been hiding away inside of me, waiting for the right time to jump out and attack. When it did, I was shocked! How long had that been hiding in there? How long had I been keeping the monster bottled up?

My brother and I were playing in the basement with our friend Chris, who lived across the street. Chris was at our house all the time. We collected and traded baseball cards, raced around the neighborhood on our bikes, and played baseball in the backyard late into the evenings, often until it was too dark to see the ball. Chris was around so much that our family called him "other brother."

On the day of this particular memory, we'd been playing together in an unfinished room in our basement, a room we called, rather unimaginatively, the "big room." We called it this because—you'll be shocked by this—it was big, easily the largest room in the basement. You'll notice that we didn't name it the "fancy room," because while it was big, it was far from fancy.

The room had concrete floors with a drain in the middle, for when rainwater leaked through the walls. There was also an ancient wooden ping-pong table with chipped green paint and a huge freezer, because grown-ups like big freezers for storing extra meat and blueberries and whatever else.

This was also the room where we played with our Star Wars action figures. We'd built elaborate fortresses out of wooden blocks my dad had brought home from work—he was a furniture parts salesman—and would make up different scenarios, none of which were remotely related to any actual Star Wars storyline. We were playing—we could do whatever we wanted!

I don't remember what initially caused the fight, but I know my brother and I got into it. Whatever it was, probably a small disagreement about something silly like who got to play with the Jabba the Hut toy, turned into something that felt like World War III. There was yelling, blocks were thrown, and a few blistering insults flew back and forth too.

Unfortunately for us, my mom was also in the basement pulling towels out of the dryer. It didn't take her long, with her motherly powers of perception, to recognize a shift from playful fun to rage. She marched into the big room, stood with her hands on her hips, and declared, "That's enough. Chris, you need to go home—*now*."

And *that* is what put my anger over the edge—an edge to which it was already dangerously close. How dare she make Chris leave! He was our best friend. It was still early on a Saturday; we couldn't survive the rest of the day without a friend to play with! In my rage I said something to my mom that I'd never said before and that I've never said since: "I hate you!"

I shouted, stormed up to my room, grabbed a miniature baseball bat we'd bought as a souvenir at a Cincinnati Reds baseball game, and smacked my favorite stuffed teddy bear in the face with it, causing his plastic eye to come off. When I saw what I'd done, I hugged him. "I'm sorry," I cried, my big tears soaking into his purple fur.

I know there was never a monster in the closet, but that day I became afraid that there was a monster in me.

Sometimes big feelings like anger, fear, and sadness surprise us. We don't always know where they come from, and they can be overwhelming, leaving us clueless about what to do with them. We try to stuff them back inside or chase them away. We'd lock them up and throw away the key if we could.

But there are lots of good ways to deal with big feelings. Sometimes talking to a grown-up who loves you can be a good place to start, especially if the big feelings are getting in the way of living your life, for instance if they are making it hard for you to concentrate in school or causing problems with your friends or family. Sometimes talking with a school counselor or a therapist might be the right way to go. There are people out there who want to help you sort through this stuff.

What I want to say here, though, is this: God is not afraid of your big feelings, even if you are. It's so easy for us to feel ashamed of them, like we're doing something wrong by having strong emotions. As a kid, when I told my mother I hated her and then hit my teddy bear, I felt so ashamed. In fact, I've never told that story before. Writing it in this book, forty years after it happened, is the first time I've ever talked about it, because I felt like there was something wrong with me. I felt like I had to hide, telling myself *no one can know about this monster in me*—especially not God. Maybe you've felt that way too.

If you have—or even if you haven't—remember: God loves you. God created you with the capacity to experience all the emotions you have. Emotions are like all the colors on a painter's palette. Some are big and loud. Some are subtle. Some of them are pretty, and some of them are honestly kind of ugly. But our lives would be so boring and gray without them.

Yes, sometimes emotions feel as explosive as opening a bottle of soda after shaking it, leading us to say and do things that hurt other people. It's good for us to reach out and get some help so we can understand them better, so we can know what to do when they feel like they are getting out of control. But big feelings aren't *wrong*—they just *are*. They are nothing to be ashamed of. They are part of us, and God loves and welcomes us just the way we are, big feelings and all.

That means you can approach any of the ways of praying you find in this book while feeling big feelings. Don't let fear or anger or sadness keep you from praying. God wants to hear from you then too! Sometimes we feel embarrassed, so we don't pray when we have big feelings, as if God would not want to hang out with us right then, as if God might see our big feelings and say, "Go home!"

But that's hogwash. It's just nonsense.

Nothing can make God hide from you. Nothing can make God send you away. Nothing can make God *want* to send you away.

You are surrounded by God's love, and there's nothing you can do to mess that up or change it.

Big feelings aren't monsters in the closet, even if they might feel that way. They are part of each one of us. They require attention and care. They need to be talked about and expressed in appropriate ways.

So along with talking to a grown-up you trust about your emotions, you can also talk to God. Before you pray, you might want to say, "God, I'm having some big feelings, and they scare me a little, but I am glad I can still be with you and that you want to be with me. Thank you."

conversation starters

- If you feel comfortable, share about a time when a big feeling surprised you. What was going on? How did it feel? Were you scared? What did you do?
- What do you tend to do with your big feelings? Hide them? Talk to someone about them? Something else? What do you want to do the next time you have a big feeling?
- Imagine sharing with God about your big feelings. Do you think that might make them feel less scary? Why or why not?

chapter five

No Right Way

Last Christmas, Mary Clare and I made Christmas cookies together. To be specific, we didn't just make any old Christmas cookies—we made my *mom's* Christmas cookies.

Every Christmas when I was growing up, and for many years after I became an adult, my mom would make dozens of thin, crispy, sugar cookies, iced in an array of colors and decorated with sprinkles. They were shaped like stars, bells, trees, and Santa boots. The boots would be covered in red icing with a white stripe to signify the fur at the top. My mom's cookies were perfect every time.

Sadly, my mom died in 2019. But every year we still make those cookies, and we use her recipe.

This time it was nine o'clock on a Friday night, the night before Christmas Eve. It had been a busy December, and it did not hit me until I walked into the kitchen that night: We hadn't made Christmas cookies yet. The reality struck me like a bolt of lightning, and I sprang into action. I pulled out the recipe then hunted through the cabinets to make sure we had the few necessary ingredients: butter, sugar, flour, salt, powdered sugar, and milk. I could only find green food coloring for the icing, but we'd make do.

I hollered for Mary Clare, "Come help me make cookies!" She joined me in the kitchen for a Friday night baking party. At each step, we read the directions my mom had written on an index card years before. We rolled out the cookies on the granite countertop, and we rolled them thin, because the recipe explicitly says *roll them thin*. I wanted these to taste *exactly* the way I remembered. To achieve that goal we had to follow the directions precisely. We had to do everything *right*.

Can you think of things in your life that are important to always do the right way? For instance, there is a right way to do math problems—you have to follow the order of operations (if you don't know what that means, ask an older sibling or a grown-up. See if they remember!). To get the right answer, you must do math the way your teacher taught you—the *right* way.

Maybe you have an older brother or sister learning to drive (Mary Clare has two older brothers learning right now). There are lots of driving rules you have to follow to be safe and to avoid seeing blue and red lights flashing behind you. Everyone wants to be safe, and no one wants a ticket. So you have to drive the *right* way.

If you've ever gone with a grown-up to vote on election day, you've seen that there are lots of rules there too. The volunteers will warn you to do everything right or your vote might not count. There's a *right* way. (If you do it the right way, a volunteer will give you an "I Voted" sticker when you leave. I guess grown-ups love stickers).

But there's something I want you to know and never forget: *Prayer doesn't work that way*. There is no rule book. There is no teacher standing over your shoulder waiting to correct you or punish you if you make a mistake. There's no prayer cop itching to give you ticket for breaking the rules. There's no volunteer waiting and ready to mark your prayer "invalid" if you don't follow every step correctly. *There are no rules!*

But if there were rules (which there aren't!) the first one would be: Relax, there's no right way to do this.

Now, there are guidelines and helpful suggestions. There's a good bit of decent advice out there about how to pray. After all, people have been praying for thousands of years. Over such a long time, people have discovered different practices that are helpful, and they've discovered other things that just get in the way.

Following these recommendations can be especially helpful when you're getting started. But when those tried-and-true suggestions get written down—in a book like this one, for instance—they can look a lot like rules. In fact, I just did a quick internet search and found several books that say they are exactly that: books full of rules about prayer. There are books with titles like *The Forgotten Rules of Prayer* and *Understanding the Rules of Prayer for Different Situations and How to Apply Them for Your Desired Outcome.*

I guess, if there *were* rules (which once again, there are not), then the second one would be: Avoid books about the rules of prayer!

When you start thinking that a guideline for prayer is a rule, a recipe you have to follow to the letter every time, you might end up spending most of your energy worrying about whether you are doing it right instead of focusing on being with God, and that completely defeats the point of the whole thing. If that happens, remember the hypothetical rule #1: Relax, there's no right way to do this.

Say that with me: *There's no right way to do this.*

Think about friendship. There's lots of good advice on how to be a friend, advice that can help us have good, strong relationships. For example, it's good to spend one-on-one time with a friend, or don't waste all the time you are spending with one friend texting someone else. But these are not hard-and-fast rules. They are guidelines, helpful reminders, and gentle nudges from people who have experienced friendship and learned a few things. It's simple, good advice.

Every friendship is different, and as helpful as good advice can be, we have to figure out how to navigate each friendship on its own.

In the same way, your relationship with God is one-of-a-kind. It will grow and become its own beautiful thing. Even if you follow helpful guidelines—and I hope you find the ones in this book helpful—eventually you'll have to find your own way. You and God will figure it out together. That's where the joy is! That's what it's all about. There is no recipe to follow, so relax and enjoy exploring prayer. Make it your own, because there's no right way. And God, for sure, isn't judging you to see if you're doing it *right*. I suspect God is simply overjoyed that you want to be friends to begin with.

After we finished decorating our cookies, Mary Clare and I admired them, all spread out on the countertop. Since we only had green food coloring, it looked more like we'd made cookies for St. Patrick's Day, but I was proud of what we'd created. I posted a picture of them on social media, and my older sister, who lives far away from us, commented on the photo: "I hope you didn't add salt." That's when I remembered that my sister also uses our mom's recipe to make Christmas cookies, but she leaves the salt out. I've never understood that. The recipe calls for just ¼ teaspoon of salt—not very much!—but I think salt is the key ingredient. I love to take a bite and taste that hint of saltiness nestled up against the sweetness—a perfect pair, *so* good.

My sister disagrees. And then I realized, when it comes to following a cookie recipe, maybe there is no right way. She can do what she wants. She's the one who is going to eat them, after all. I just hope she never sends me any without salt.

Mary Clare says . . .

Recently, I've been getting into tennis. Every weekday during summer vacation from noon to two, I participate in a tennis clinic run by my school's tennis coach. One day, I asked him why my wrist was hurting and he explained that it was because of the strain I put on those muscles when I served because my form was wrong. So, at my next lesson, we worked on my serve.

I had to completely change the way I was serving. I tried to follow the new steps he taught me as closely as I could: Shift your balance from the front foot to the back, throw the ball straight up and to the right, and, at the exact right time on the ball's way back down, throw your arm and racket to the right and hit the ball on the back so that you get the perfect mix of spin and strength on your serve. Then—and this is what I was especially struggling with—right after contact with the ball, rotate your forearm and let your arm fall across your body, eventually tucking your left arm across your chest under your right arm.

So, I tried it out. Toss, hit . . . into the net. *Ugh.* Toss, hit . . . too far to the left. *Agh.* Toss, hit . . . way too long. *Yikes.* I tried so many times, but I couldn't get the hang of it. My coach could tell that I was getting frustrated. "Are you a perfectionist?" he asked me. I hesitated and thought of all the times in my life when I try to do things the right way: writing essays for school (they have to follow the formula exactly), drawing people (the proportions need to look exactly right, otherwise they'll look like aliens), and even drafting text messages to friends (if I don't say this exactly right, they'll get the wrong message!). "Yes," I responded. He told me—and I don't know if this is true or if he was just trying to make a point—that even professional tennis players make mistakes 50% of the time, and the hardest part is to learn from them, fix them, and do it a little better the next time. He told me the biggest part of the game was making mistakes and growing from them. Even so, there's still a right way to do things, and you have to try over and over to get it right.

Now, unlike a tennis serve, I'm discovering there's no "right" way to pray. Sure, there are guidelines you can follow, but if it doesn't work for you, that doesn't mean you're doing it wrong. There are no rules. As a perfectionist myself, this is hard to grapple with; I want there to be steps to follow, a list to check off, or a way to *know* that I'm doing it right. At the same time, it's freeing to know that no matter how I pray, I'll never, ever do it wrong. Just like tennis, I can practice praying over and over until I figure out what's just right for me. And God is okay if what's right for me isn't right for you. God is just happy that you're spending time with God, and *that's* the right thing to do.

conversation starters

- Have you ever felt like you had to pray the *right* way? Did you ever worry that you were not very good at it? How did that affect the way you thought about prayer?
- Talk together about some ways you've been taught you *should* pray. How has it felt trying to pray this way? Are there ways of praying you'd like to try instead?
- Imagine that prayer is like a page in a coloring book, and you've been invited to color outside of the lines. How does that feel? Exciting? Intimidating? Why?

chapter six

Answered Prayer

Sometimes when we get home from church on Sunday, Mary Clare has an idea pop into her head. In fact, it happens much more often than sometimes. This idea pops into her head at the alarmingly frequent rate of every week. This could be because we don't get home from church until around 1:00 p.m.—my wife and I are pastors, so we are often the last ones to leave the building. By that time, we are all hungry. And that's when Mary Clare voices her idea: "Can we go to ABC for lunch, *please?*" Picture a pleading face with hands clasped as in prayer. Picture a thirteen-year-old positively begging.

ABC is shorthand for a coffee shop called Aspinwall Beans & Cream, and Mary Clare badly wants their bacon, lettuce, and tomato sandwich on an everything bagel, with guacamole slathered on for an extra seventy cents. Either that, or she wants tuna salad on an everything bagel, with bacon added for an extra dollar. Or, if she's really feeling ambitious, she'll beg me to order a BLT while she orders a tuna salad sandwich, and then we'll share so she can have the best of both worlds.

She says it again and again. "Can we, *please?*" She looks at me with her big blue eyes while she rubs her tummy, as if taking her out to lunch is the only way to cure her hunger. Eventually, she wears me down until I sigh and say, "Okay." She doesn't always receive the answer she wants, but often she does. (I bet you have your own strategies to get the grown-ups in your life to say yes to what *you* want too. Am I right? I thought so.)

When Mary Clare does this, I'm reminded of a story Jesus tells in the Gospel of Luke, one of the parables he crafted to help his disciples understand an important point. It goes something like this:

There was a judge, and he was not a good man. He didn't care about God, and he didn't care about other people. There was also a woman, and she had a problem with someone. We don't know what the problem was, but we're made to believe she was in the right and the other person was in the wrong. She comes to the judge and demands, "Grant me justice. Do the right thing. Make the situation right." The judge refuses, so she comes back a second time. Again, he refuses. Then she comes back, then she comes back again, and then she comes back once again, over and over and over until the judge is tired of the woman's begging. "She just won't give up," the judge thinks, "and I'm sick of it! I don't care at all about her—I really don't care about anything—but if I give her what she wants, at least she'll stop bothering me." So finally, he gives her what she's asking for, so she'll leave him alone (see Luke 18:1-8).

I share the story about Mary Clare wearing me down to get lunch along with the parable Jesus told about the woman who wore a judge down until he relented to make the same point: God is not like that. God is not like me or like the judge. God *loves* to hear what is on your heart. God *desires* for you to come to God with your wants and needs. God is *eager* to respond to the needs of God's people.

It's good for us to bring to God our petitions (that's just a fancy word that means prayers asking God for something for ourselves) and intercessions (that's a fancy word that means prayers asking God for something for other people). Asking God for things—for a safe family vacation, to feel less anxious before a test, for that new kid in class to notice you and be your friend—is not all prayer is about, but it's part of it. And God is not like an unjust judge or a begrudging dad: God doesn't just *give in* eventually. God finds joy in hearing our prayers and answering them.

There are times when we pray about something, and we see visible results. Those are the times when it feels like God has answered our prayer. But if God finds joy in answering our prayers, why don't we see it more often? Why don't we see answered prayer *all the time*? You may pray for a sick pet, one you have loved for years, but the pet keeps getting worse. Maybe you pray to get a good grade on a test, and you get a C+, or you pray for a parent who has lost a job, but you can still see the worry on their face.

I wish I had a clear answer to this question, but I don't. Sometimes we see the answer to our prayers and it's obvious; sometimes we don't see anything at all. Sometimes we see an answer to our prayers, but it's been such a long time or it's such an unexpected answer that we don't notice that it's an answer to our prayer at all!

You see, there is a mystery hidden at the heart of our relationship with God. There are some questions that aren't meant to be answered; rather, they are meant to be lived with. I think this *why* question is one of them. I know I don't have answers, but I do have some suggestions about how to keep praying in the face of this reality.

First, pray. It's that simple: Just pray. Bring your requests and intercessions and wants and needs and hopes and dreams to God. Bring it all to God. True, God is not like a candy dispenser that gives us whatever we want. But God is also not like an unjust judge who wants us to go away. What kind of friend would God be if God didn't want to hear what we need or want? What kind of friend would God be if God didn't want to know what we are thinking about and hoping for? So just keep sharing it all, keep talking to God. Pray.

Second, keep your eyes open. There are times when a prayer gets answered in an obvious way, but sometimes we see God work in less obvious ways—sometimes in surprising ways, sometimes in hidden ways.

Sometimes we can look back months or years later and see how God was answering our prayer though we didn't notice it at the time. We might even find ourselves thanking God that God didn't answer the prayer the way we'd hoped. After all, God knows what is good for us and those we love better than we do.

Finally, trust. Keep trusting that when we don't see what we hope to see, God's love is still at work, mysterious though it may be. When something doesn't turn out the way we want (our pet doesn't recover, we earn a poor grade on that test, our parent struggles to find a job), these things are still true:

God is there. God is at work. God loves you (and that pet, and the teacher who graded the test, and the worried parent). And God is delighted that you are still sharing your hopes, dreams, and desires through prayer. Your relationship is growing and getting stronger every time you do.

conversation starters

- Have you ever prayed for something, and it seemed like the prayer was answered? What was that like?
- Have you ever prayed for something, but then nothing happened? How did that make you feel?
- How do you find it easiest to share with your thoughts, feelings, and desires with God? By praying at bedtime? Journaling? Talking with God when you're anxious? Some other way?

chapter seven

Open, Available, Responsive

On the day I'm writing this a new Zelda video game has just been released. Though I have played many video games in my life, I do not know about this release because I am a gamer or because I plan to play it myself. I know because my son wants this game.

When Nintendo first became popular in the late 1980s, my brother and I were middle schoolers. Initially, we had no interest. We didn't ask for one from our parents, and we didn't hope for one either. We were neutral. Santa Claus, however, decided we did need one, so on Christmas morning, wrapped beneath the tree next to the gloves, scarves, and sweaters that Santa would bring us every year, there was a brand-new Nintendo. As it turned out, we loved it! We played *Duck Hunt*, *Mike Tyson's Punch Out*, *Super Mario Brothers*, *Top Gun* (boy was it hard to land those jets on an aircraft carrier; I can still see my plane sliding off the ship and into the ocean), and the original *Legend of Zelda*, which came out in 1986.

But by the time we were in high school, we'd stopped playing.

Then, when my sons were young, video games came back into my life. Since the first day they played Super Mario Brothers, they have stayed interested in video games. Now I have an eighteen-year-old son named

Silas who has been anticipating the release of a new Zelda game for two years. A few months ago, a trailer for the new game dropped. Not only has he watched the trailer a thousand times (and made me watch it too), but he has also spent hours watching shows and reading articles online about the trailer—*the trailer!*

And today is finally the day. After school, he will drive to the store where he pre-ordered the game and where a copy should be waiting behind the counter with his name on it. Finally, he will get to bring it home and play the game he's been waiting for. I'm sure the game is waiting more patiently for him than he has been waiting for it.

Now, imagine that when Silas arrives at the store, he notices that all the lights are off and sees a sign that reads "Closed." If it's past the store's closing time, he'll be frustrated with himself for arriving late. But how will he feel if he gets there during regular business hours and they're closed without any explanation?

He'll be angry! *He. Wants. His. Game!*

Let's say he returns the next morning, having slept badly because he was so annoyed the night before, but now the sign says "Open," the lights are on, and the door is unlocked. He breathes a sigh of relief, walks in, and looks around for a clerk to help him. But he can't find one. They're open, but no one is there! Again, he leaves, but now he's even more annoyed.

So, he decides to come back an hour later. This time things have to work out, right? He walks into the store and, again, doesn't see anyone, but he does hear a noise coming from behind a door marked "Employees Only." He approaches the door and overhears the clerk talking to his buddy on FaceTime. He realizes that they are talking about how great the new Zelda game is! So Silas opens the door, and the employee looks at him and holds up a finger and mouths, "Just a minute," but he never does come out to help. This time, the store is open, an employee is there, available to help Silas, but he isn't responsive. Once again, my son storms out, shaking his fists in the air.

But he's willing to give it one final try. This time, the sign says "Open," and when he walks in, the clerk working the afternoon shift is standing behind the counter. She smiles and greets him, "Good afternoon to you, friend! How might I help you on this lovely day?" and Silas thinks, *Do people really talk like that?* But it's going way better than when he was here before. He feels hopeful—he might actually get his game. He says he's here to pick up a Zelda game he ordered and tells the clerk his name. The clerk says, "Of course, let me retrieve that for you right away," and two minutes later, Silas is skipping out of the store, game clutched in his hand, daydreaming about spending the rest of the weekend in video game bliss.

The first time the store was closed, not *open*.

The second time it was open, but no employees were *available*.

The third time the store was open and a clerk was available, but he was distracted and not *responsive*.

Finally, the fourth time the store was open, the clerk was available, *and* she was responsive to him.

Open. Available. Responsive.

When I talk to people about prayer, I use these three words all the time. I tell them over and over, "Prayer helps us to become open, available, and responsive to God." Each word indicates a deeper level of our openness to God and to God's work in our lives. When we pray, we can ask ourselves: Am I approaching prayer with an attitude of openness, a spirit of availability, and a willingness to respond? Those are questions you'll want to consider as you begin this journey of prayer.

Whatever prayer practice you are using (and there are many in this book), it can be helpful to take a few moments to express to God your hopes for that particular time of prayer. You might say something like, "Dear God, in this time of prayer, I long to be open, available, and responsive to your presence in my life." You are free to use these exact words, but eventually you'll find the words that are right for you to express your unique desire to be open to God in the moment.

And here's the great thing: It's not just during specific times of prayer that we can seek to be open, available, and responsive to God. We can approach our *whole life* that way. You can pray this prayer for openness before *any* activity.

- Before a family vacation: *God, in the time away with my family, help me notice you and be available to your presence. Help me see you in my family members and the fun we have together, and help me respond to you by showing love.*
- Before math class: *God, I know you are here—even at school! I need to focus on math right now, but deep in my spirit, I want to be available to you. Who knows? There might be something you want to show me even as I do these math problems.*
- Before a sporting event: *God, you made my body, and you are present as I run around and use it. May I be open and available to experiencing your presence through the wonderful gift of my body! May my joy in this game be a response to the gift of this opportunity.*

You can even say this to God before playing Zelda. I mean, sure, why not?

conversation starters

- Have you ever wanted something really badly, only to discover that it was unavailable? How did that make you feel?
- If God wants a relationship with us, how do you think God might feel when we are not open to that relationship?
- What are some things that can get in the way of people being open, available, and responsive to God?

chapter eight

Prayer Is Natural

Have you ever met someone who is a gifted athlete or musician? Maybe you've heard someone say, "They're a natural." This is what we say when it looks like a person is doing something—swishing a basketball, launching a home run, playing the violin—that comes easily to them, as if they were born knowing how to do it.

A few days ago, one of Mary Clare's friends was featured on the radio playing a piece of classical piano music. He played it flawlessly. After he finished, the broadcaster said, "I understand you know well the person who wrote that piece of music." He replied, "Yes, I came up with that while I was messing around at the piano yesterday." My jaw dropped open. *He* wrote *that? Yesterday?* I thought to myself. My very next thought was: *He's a natural.*

Now, when we say that one person is a natural, what does that suggest about the rest of us? You guessed it—it suggests that we're *not* naturals. I can assure you, I am not a natural athlete (just ask my kids). I could have been a decent tennis player if I'd devoted myself to the sport when I was younger and taken lessons. I did take golf lessons, which helped me make the middle school golf team—barely. I gave basketball a shot when I was in fifth grade, and it didn't go well. I was slow, afraid to touch the ball, and always relieved when the coach put me back on the bench.

It's not a great idea to divide people into categories like this, but it's something we say, and it's true that some skills come more easily to some people. But it's dangerous if we begin to think this way when it comes to prayer—that some people are just naturals and some people aren't.

Because when it comes to prayer, we are *all* naturals.

Pause and read that last sentence again.

Here's what I mean: God made us to want a connection with God, to love God, and to live lives that move in the direction of God. We are created to have a relationship with God, to even have a friendship with God. Prayer is one of the ways we express and build that relationship. We are made for it. It's part of us. It's natural—just like fish are made to swim, birds to fly, and bees to buzz annoyingly around your food at a picnic.

And prayer isn't just natural for a few special people. It's that way for everyone. No one can read the words "Prayer is natural" and say, "No, that doesn't apply to me!" That's just how it is, even for you.

Scientists still don't fully understand how birds know where to go when they migrate. They've figured out that birds use things like the sun, stars, and magnetic fields to help them, but the whole process is still a mystery. Some birds fly thousands of miles to the same place every year without getting lost. That seems miraculous to me—especially since I sometimes get lost just walking around a grocery store. It's like birds have a built-in compass that points them in the right direction and helps them find their way. It's just natural for them.

You have an inner compass too, and it points you to God, the source of your life and the love that created you. Loving God and moving toward friendship with God through prayer is natural.

With that said, I can hear you asking: Then why doesn't it *feel* natural?

Maybe you've already tried some of the exercises in this book, and they felt tricky, maybe even downright hard. Maybe when you tried, you felt restless or distracted or bored; maybe you kept reaching for your phone. Maybe you felt like you'd rather be doing something—or anything—else. FaceTiming a friend, for instance—*that* feels natural. Prayer? Not so much.

Here's the truth: I feel the same way sometimes—actually, a lot of the time.

Remember, God is a mystery. We can't just call God or reach out and give God a hug like we can one of our friends. We can't feel God's presence the way we can feel the presence of the person next to us on the school bus or a grandparent who comes to visit for the weekend. Prayer requires trust: trust that God is there, present, listening and loving us, even when we don't feel it.

Sometimes prayer feels good, and we might even sense God's nearness. It's really nice when that happens! But at other times—especially when we are just starting out—prayer can feel awkward. At those times, it doesn't provide immediate satisfaction, at least not the same cozy satisfaction of lounging on a couch while watching a movie with friends at a slumber party.

But keep this in mind too: You are here, right now, thinking about prayer, talking to grown-ups about prayer, maybe even reading parts of this book for yourself. I suspect you are not doing it because someone has promised you a prize if you do. I bet that there is a longing in you, that deep down you are curious. Maybe you're starting to realize that more stuff—more toys, clothes, games, electronics, money—is not going to satisfy you, that it's never going to be enough. So here you are, asking questions about prayer, figuring out how to find a home in God's love.

You know what all that means? It means your inner compass is pointing you in the right direction. That longing, those questions, your curiosity—they are the first signs that prayer is natural.

So, prayer is natural . . .

And it can be confusing . . .

And it can feel hard sometimes . . .

And it can feel good sometimes . . .

And all of these things can be true at the same time.

Here's the good news, though—God is patient. God isn't going anywhere. God isn't going to stop loving you, not ever, ever, ever, ever, ever. God isn't going to stop calling to you, inviting you into the safest embrace you can imagine. God isn't going to stop wanting to be your closest friend, and God's love will always be your home.

There's no rush. Take your time. Explore. Be curious. Ask for guidance when it's confusing and remember: God's got your back.

You've got this, kid.

You're a natural.

Mary Clare says . . .

A few years ago, my favorite music teacher from school started to give me private piano lessons. I was so excited to become a phenomenal pianist. I wanted to effortlessly play rich pieces that made people stop in awe. I wanted to piece together chords and words and make my own songs. I wanted to do so much with the piano, but for the two months I took lessons, all I did was practice scales and short, two-line melodies. Over and over. I was never able to easily write my own songs or perform beautiful works of music in those two months, so I quit. I was not a natural. I would never be a natural. And I didn't have the patience to become "good" at the piano.

Sometimes prayer doesn't feel natural to me either. On occasion, praying feels like I'm pretending to be a master at something that I know nothing about. It's okay to struggle with prayer, but that isn't a reason to quit. I'm learning you don't have to be a master at prayer to be a natural. All you have to do is simply spend time with God, which is, ultimately, the most natural thing we can do.

conversation starters

- Is there anything you do that feels natural to you? What makes it feel that way?
- Has praying ever felt natural to you? If so, what was that like? Has praying ever felt *not* natural to you? If so, what was that like?
- Does it make a difference to know that praying is natural, especially in those times when it seems confusing? What difference do you think it makes?

chapter nine

God the Initiator

The word *initiate* means "to start" or "to get something started." Imagine you have a younger brother who ate the last jellybean from your Easter candy. You might *initiate* a conversation with him—and when you do, I wouldn't want to be that little brother! If the conversation turns into a fight—maybe there's some yelling or a few threats (let's hope not)—a parent will eventually step in and tell you to stop. Your brother, pointing an accusing finger in your direction, will protest, "They started it!" to which you would likely respond, "No I didn't! He started it when he ate my last piece of Easter candy!"

At first, you were arguing about eating the final jellybean, but now you're arguing about who started the *argument* about eating the final jellybean. You are now debating who was the *initiator*.

That story might not sound like a story that connects to prayer, but I assure you it does.

I typically pray in the morning, but I struggle to get out of bed in the mornings too. I really like the comfort of my bed, and I hate to leave it. In my experience, a lot of kids are the same. As I write these words, it's morning and I've already prayed. Mary Clare, on the other hand, is lying in her bed, curled up beneath plush covers and surrounded by a small collection of stuffed animals. This is true even though I jostled her fifteen minutes ago and told her it was time to wake up. I had the *initiative*—hey, it's another version of that word!—to get up, and she's still trying to find some.

Because it's so hard for me to get out of bed, praying in the morning feels like hard work. My inner tired middle schooler wants to hit snooze again, roll over, and ignore the part of me that says, "It's time to wake up and head downstairs to pray." (By the way, I just heard footsteps upstairs which means Mary Clare has successfully exited her bed. Initiative!)

Deciding to spend time with God clearly takes some initiative. We have to *do* something to start praying. At least it feels that way.

But here's my question for you: What if we think about this whole business of initiative differently? What if *God* is the true *initiator*? What if God "started it"?

When it comes to developing a relationship with God, God is the one who gets things started. We see this in the life of Jesus. When Jesus called his first disciples to follow him, they were just doing their jobs as fishermen. They were not looking for Jesus, and there is no reason to think they wanted to quit their jobs. Then Jesus walked up and said, "Come, follow me." Guess what? *They did!* They dropped their nets, turned their backs on their boats, and followed (See Mark 1:16-20).

Jesus took the initiative, and they responded.

There's a story in the gospel of Luke I have always loved. It's about a woman who had a condition that left her completely bent over. She was stuck staring at the ground. One day she was standing in the back of the worship space while Jesus was teaching. It's possible she was trying to stay out of the way, trying to avoid being seen. Back then, people were sometimes blamed for their own physical struggles. Some people would wag a finger and say, "You must have done something very wrong for God to let this happen to you!"

This wrongheaded way of thinking upset Jesus—he knew it was unfair to blame people for the bad things that happened in their lives. He looked at her, hiding in the back, and he called her forward. Imagine how surprised she must have been! Then he laid his hands on her crooked spine—such a lovely gesture, particularly since it's likely no one else wanted to touch her—and his tender love healed her. In response, the woman immediately stood up straight, threw her hands in the air, and praised God. I wish I could have been there to see that. I get goosebumps just thinking about it—how shocked she must have been when Jesus called to her! What joy must have been flooding her when Jesus set her free from her condition (see Luke 13:10-17)!

This story is about Jesus as the initiator.

Believe it or not, it's the same way with prayer. Honestly, it's the same with everything about your relationship with God. God is the initiator. God's love gets this journey of prayer started for you. God is reaching out to you because God wants to be your friend. Sometimes prayer feels easy; sometimes it feels tricky (especially in the mornings!). Either way, it's a response to God's love that is already active in your life.

God is at work in our lives, even if we don't notice it right away. God is waking us up because we spend much of our lives asleep to God's presence. God is nudging us, like a parent sitting on the edge of their child's bed in the morning, gently whispering, "It's time to get up. Why don't we spend some time together today? Nothing would make me happier."

Prayer isn't what *we* do to start a relationship with God. It's not as if God is sitting back with arms crossed just waiting for us to make something happen. Prayer is a response—our response to God, who is already present in our lives, initiating this relationship of love.

Below you'll find two of my favorite quotes from two of my favorite writers. I'm going to offer them to you without any explanation. They're meant for you to chew on and think about. You can have a conversation with a grown-up about them. You can memorize them, tuck them into the back of your mind, and carry them around with you for a while, letting their meaning slowly sink deep into your heart. You can take these two quotes and savor them slowly, like they are the only two jellybeans left, and you want to make them last:

"[T]he living Christ within us is the initiator and we are the responders. . . And all our apparent initiative is already a response . . ." —Thomas Kelly[6]

". . . God is closer than we think, [and] there is no path to God that is not first God's path to us." —John Mogabgab[7]

conversation starters

- When does it feel like you have to take the initiative to pray? When does it feel easy and when does it feel hard?
- Have you ever sensed that God was at work in your life? Have you ever felt like you were responding to God? What was that like?
- How might our feelings about prayer shift if we think of prayer as a response to God's love?

chapter ten

Prayer Doesn't Accomplish Anything

At the school where I teach, I have a lot of students. Unlike you, all of my students are grown-ups, many of whom are preparing to be ministers—pastors, preachers, chaplains—and some of them already are. My students are busy people. Some have families—kids to get ready for school in the morning or babies to feed, bathe, and put to bed. I've seen many of these babies on screen during our online classes, and I've heard even more of them crying off screen; lots of my students have jobs and attend class in the evenings.

Many of them have long to do lists. There is a lot they need to accomplish. Sometimes they struggle with balancing it all. This occasionally leads them to argue with me when I tell them that they should take time to pray even though prayer doesn't accomplish anything—it doesn't get anything done.

"Think of prayer as wasting time with God," I say. They almost can't handle it. "We don't have time to waste with anyone—not even God!" they respond.

I can appreciate their struggle. Prayer doesn't get a sermon written (something I have to do every week) or a homework assignment finished (something they, and you, have to do every week). Prayer doesn't fix a leaky roof or shop for the groceries or get a kid picked up from school. (I mean, if you ever had to wait for someone to pick you up from school, you'd be at least a little frustrated if you ended up walking home because they had to make time to pray, right?)

You can add "pray" to your to-do list and check it off every day, but even then, it won't make you feel particularly accomplished. It doesn't offer the same satisfaction as finishing your homework on a Saturday morning then feeling relaxed the rest of the weekend because you knocked out a big task. And so, these grown-up students struggle.

You're younger than my students, so I'm guessing that you haven't yet forgotten how to relax—how to hang out, how to simply do . . . nothing. Trust me, that's a skill. You still know how to enjoy a lazy Saturday morning lying around in bed, then wandering into the family room to watch a movie, play a video game, or text with your friends. You're not doing anything really, not accomplishing anything—and you're loving it!

So, maybe you won't freak out like my adult students when you learn that prayer doesn't accomplish anything.

But even if you buy in to what I'm saying, there still might be a piece of you, in the back of your mind, that hopes prayer does something. *If I pray*, you might be thinking, *it will make a grown-up in my life happy. It might convince them I'm mature and responsible. Impressive, even. That would be something.*

Maybe praying *will* impress an adult, and if that's the reason you are interested in prayer, that's fine. In fact, anything that gets you started is fine. You can't start anywhere but where you are.

But what I'm concerned about is something else we might hope prayer accomplishes, something hidden so deep within us that we never put it into words. Even if we don't say it, it's still there, lurking: We think prayer will get *God* to like us. We think that *God* will be impressed with us. That wouldn't be so bad, would it? To have God, the creator of the universe, creator of *everything* from tiny bacteria to distant galaxies, look at us and say, "Wow, (your name here) is praying—now that's impressive. Little more of that and I could start liking that kid. I'm going to give them a gold star, and if they pray again tomorrow, *another* gold star. Way to go, kid!"

Hidden in that secret place in our hearts, a place no one else knows about, many of us hold onto a hope: that prayer will get God to notice us, to believe in us, to love us.

But prayer couldn't possibly accomplish *that.*

And the reason is really quite simple: God *already* does.

There's nothing *you* can do to get God to like you, accept you, or approve of you *because God already does.* God is love, and God surrounds you completely with love.

When you were just a slobbery, whiny, poopy baby, who wouldn't go to sleep and cried all night long, God already liked you, loved you, and accepted you.

When you were a toddler throwing temper tantrums, screaming and crying in the aisle of the grocery store and embarrassing to death whatever grown-ups were with you, God already liked you, loved you, and accepted you.

When you were in school learning to make your letters and getting them all wrong, writing a "g" that looked like a "y" and an "R" that looked like a "P," God didn't care about the printed letters on the page. God already liked you, loved you, and accepted you.

And God still does. Got the picture?

In the first chapter of this book, we talked about friendship with God. I wrote about how Jesus, after he had washed his disciples' feet, said, "I no longer call you servants . . . but I have called you friends" (John 15:15). Well, here's something you need to know: Those first disciples of Jesus, the twelve apostles—they were legit screw-ups. They failed repeatedly to understand what Jesus was talking about. They bickered among themselves about who was the best and most important. One of them was just about to betray Jesus, another was about to deny he ever knew Jesus, and most of them would abandon Jesus when he needed them the most. If you were going to pick a group of people to like because of what they'd accomplished or what they'd done for you, you would *never* pick these twelve.

But Jesus did, and he said he wanted to be their friend. He loved them, liked them, and accepted them without ever thinking about what they had accomplished (not much) or had failed to accomplish (quite a lot).

They never did anything to earn his favor. They didn't have to. He already loved them.

God enjoys your company. God likes to be with you. God has opened the door to God's own life and said, "Come on in. You belong with me. Let's hang out."

Maybe prayer is just the word we use for hanging out with God, for walking through the door of love that God has already opened. Pretty cool, eh?

If you are like my grown-up students, then that will be harder to do than you think. When you have a lot of things to get done, "wasting time" with God is hard to do. But I tell you: It's what you were made for, so give it a shot. Find some time to spend with God. You'll have plenty of time to do your homework, practice the tuba, and redecorate your bedroom later. There's time enough to waste a little with God.

conversation starters

- Some people struggle with the idea that prayer doesn't accomplish anything. How do you feel about it?
- How does it feel to you to think of prayer as just hanging out with God?
- Have you ever felt like you had to earn God's favor or acceptance? How does it feel to be told you don't have to because God already loves and accepts you?

chapter eleven

There's More, So Much More

When I was in fourth grade, my teacher was named Mr. Walker. Mr. Walker wore glasses, had a bushy beard that covered most of his face, and had a shiny bald spot on the top of his head. Mr. Walker also demanded an orderly classroom. He took teaching seriously, and he didn't put up with foolishness. When we were learning our multiplication tables, he took on the role of an army general, drilling us with flashcards. If you'd asked me then to describe Mr. Walker, I would have probably said he was mean. I envied my fourth-grade friends in the neighboring classroom who had Mrs. Broadwell as a teacher. There was always laughter spilling from next door which told me they were having much more fun than I was.

A year later, when I was in fifth grade, I played on the school basketball team. Guess who coached the team? That's right—Mr. Walker. Every day after school, I was in the gym running basketball drills with a bunch of other sweaty boys—all of whom were better than I was. And every day after school, there was Mr. Walker, standing on the sideline, barking orders, his hands planted on his hips, an elastic band securing his glasses to his head as if *he* were the one who might get them knocked off while scurrying for a rebound. *Why couldn't Mrs. Broadwell coach basketball*? I wondered.

That was forty years ago. Recently, a church in my hometown asked me to talk with a small group about a book I had written. The group had read the book, and some of the people in the group remembered me from when I was younger. When I saw the participants for the discussion, I recognized some of them: a woman I had gone to high school with, a woman who had been friends with my older brother, and in the back, a much older man who looked vaguely familiar. It took me a few moments to realize that it was Mr. Walker.

My heart skipped a beat, and I felt a little nervous—that is, until his face broke into the warmest smile I'd ever seen, a smile that beamed right through his thinning white beard. He laughed a hearty laugh and said, "It's good to see you, Roger!" *Maybe this isn't Mr. Walker*, I thought. But it was. Over the hour that I spent with that group, Mr. Walker laughed, told stories about his life, and shared about his faith in God. It was beautiful.

My early encounters with Mr. Walker, back when he was my teacher and coach, *were not the whole truth about him*. There was another side to Mr. Walker I'd never seen—gentle, caring, funny, a person of deep faith. I suspect those characteristics were present in the classroom too, but I was too busy focusing on how serious he was to notice. There was more to Mr. Walker than my earliest experiences with him let on—so much more.

I share this story to make a simple point: It's not any different with prayer—your first experiences of prayer don't tell the whole story.

It's likely you have some early memories of praying. Maybe your family says a prayer of thanks before dinner. Maybe you memorized the Lord's Prayer when you were small and recited it every Sunday in church. Maybe you got on your knees every night before going to bed and asked God to forgive you for the things you'd done wrong that day or to help you with challenges you'd have to face the next.

We may be tempted to think that our first experiences of prayer tell us *everything* there is to know—as if they fully reveal the mystery of prayer.

If our earliest memory is thanking God for food, we might think prayer is *all* about giving thanks. If our earliest memory is reciting the Lord's Prayer on Sunday mornings, we might think prayer is *all* about repeating prayers that we have memorized. If our earliest memory is being bored by a pastor wearing fancy robes and praying long-winded prayers in church, then we might think *all* of prayer is listening to ministers pray on our behalf.[8]

Any one of these things *can* be a part of prayer—giving thanks, reciting memorized prayers, allowing others to pray on our behalf—but don't let yourself get stuck thinking that this is all there is to prayer. Much like a person—like Mr. Walker—prayer is a mystery and has many sides and multiple characteristics. It can take a lifetime (or longer) to explore them all.

Starting off on a journey of prayer means saying, "I'm glad I've had this experience with prayer so far and know something about what prayer is, but I'm not going to confuse what little I know about prayer with the whole mystery of prayer. Prayer is much bigger and more interesting than I can possibly imagine. I know there is a great deal more for me to discover. If God is infinite (and God is) then prayer must be infinite too!"

Your early experiences with prayer tell you something, but they don't tell you everything. So, stay open and stay curious. There's more to discover.

So. Much. More.

Mary Clare says . . .

When I was much younger, I would sometimes wake up before the sky was light, sleepily walk downstairs to my dad's office, and find him sitting in an armchair, eyes closed, earbuds in, listening to a prayer app on his phone with a cup of coffee on the side table. I'd tap him on the shoulder, his eyes would open, and he'd smile as I curled up in his lap. "What are you doing so early in the morning?" I'd ask. And he would respond, "Praying." I could always smell the coffee on his breath. Once I decided to leave him alone, I would watch him put his earbuds back in and close his eyes again. I learned that this was his time with God.

This was one of my first experiences with individual prayer. I thought it had to be quiet, early in the morning, and very, very still. So sometimes I would try to wake up in the morning and read my Bible just like my dad would, but many times I'd fall back asleep or get distracted.

Over years of trying to replicate his way of praying, I learned that it just doesn't work for me. I would struggle because I thought this was the *only* way to pray alone since it was the first way I'd ever seen it done. But that's not the case.

My dad still wakes up most days before the sun, wishes me a good morning, and goes downstairs to pray before I even leave for school. It works for him. I've learned, though, that there are *so many other* ways to pray. It can be quiet and still like how my dad prays, but it can also be loud, it can be on the go, or it can be in a bright place. Prayer is not defined by the first way you've ever seen someone pray. Prayer can be your own way of spending time with God. And it's okay if that's different from what you used to believe prayer was.

conversation starters

- Talk about your earliest memories of prayer. What do those memories tell you about prayer?
- What are some aspects of prayer you are aware of now that you weren't aware of during your earliest experiences of prayer?
- What more are you hoping to learn or experience about prayer as you get older? In what ways does prayer still feel mysterious to you?

chapter twelve

When and Where

Have you ever known someone who really wanted to do a certain thing, but then just . . . didn't do it? It's strange, don't you think? Why would someone *not* do the thing they wanted to do, especially if it's within their power to do it?

But then, we all do this from time to time. I've done it myself. I'll wake up on a Saturday morning, pour a cup of coffee, sit down with my wife, Ginger, and she'll ask, "What are you going to do today?" Then I'll answer, "I want to go to the gym and exercise today." I know how great I feel after walking vigorously for forty minutes on the treadmill and then stretching out on the floor—I feel energized and invigorated. I sleep better at night when I'm exercising regularly. It's what I want to do! Then, before I know it, the day is over, the gym is closed, and I never so much as pulled on my sneakers. I wanted to go, but I didn't.

I bet you can think of similar examples from your own life. Maybe you want to get better at playing the tuba, and you tell yourself that this week you are going to practice more. (Your band teacher will be very happy; the people living in your house . . . not so much.) You tell yourself that you're going to play scales every day, practice the song you're learning in band that has that funky tuba part, and prepare for the tuba solo auditions. But by the time Friday rolls around, you realize you haven't practiced once.

We all do it. It turns out thinking about doing something, and even wanting to do it, is not enough to get it done.

We face the same challenge with prayer. I meet many, many people who desperately want to pray but don't. These are the kind of people who would buy a book on prayer (like this one!), promise themselves they will read it to kickstart their praying, and then three months later find themselves dusting it off as it sits, unread, on the coffee table.

There are lots of reasons we might avoid the things we want to do, like praying, but I'm not going to go into them. That's not the point of this chapter. Instead, I want to offer a piece of advice that can help you overcome some of those obstacles, so you'll be more likely to do the things you actually want to do, like pray.

My advice is simple: Establish ahead of time *where* you are going to do the activity and *when* you are going to do it. I would even suggest writing it down.[9]

For a long time, I thought about writing this book, but I only got started when I scribbled on a notecard one night before bed, "Tomorrow, after I make my coffee in the morning, I will work on *Praying Their Way* in my chair in the basement." It worked—I began writing once I made a date with myself. Simply knowing *when* and *where* I was going to write helped me to do it. Deciding when and where can help with practicing the tuba as well, or anything else you want to do. Reluctant tuba players might want to declare, "Today I will practice my tuba when I get home from school in my bedroom." It really works!

Maybe you're discussing this book with a grown-up in your life—a parent, children's or youth minister, or another adult who cares about you—and you've flipped through some of the prayer practices and thought that some of them look interesting. Maybe you've talked about some of these short chapters on prayer and thought, "Yes, I'd like to grow in friendship with God," because you've discovered within yourself a desire for a deeper connection with God.

Well, first: *Yay for you!* That's a great thing to notice! How wonderful that you desire to know God and want to pray! If your arms are flexible enough, pat yourself on the back. If they aren't, get someone else to pat you on the back. This is something to celebrate!

But if you want to *actually* pray, you might find it helpful to ask: When would be a good time to pray (remember, you don't need a lot of time, especially to begin with) and where would be a good place? It's likely you already know some places and times that would *not* be good, for instance, in the family room in the evening when your parents are watching the news or while eating lunch in the cafeteria at school. Of course, you can pray at these times and in these places, but when you're starting out, finding places and times where you won't be interrupted or distracted can be helpful.

The best time and place will be different for each person. Maybe it's at the desk in your bedroom after you get home from school. Maybe it's sitting on the edge of your bed after brushing your teeth and before going to bed. Maybe it's while riding the school bus in the morning. There are no right times and there is not one right place. You get to decide. But simply knowing when and where you are going to pray clears some of the obstacles out of the way and increases the chances that you will.

When Mary Clare was in eighth grade she had a friend. A boy in her grade wanted to hang out with that friend because the boy had a crush on her. In other words, he wanted to have a date with her. The boy was also Mary Clare's friend, and he was texting Mary Clare, asking her if she thought the girl he had a crush on would say yes to a date. Mary Clare assured him that the girl would, and eventually the boy found the courage to ask Mary Clare's friend on a date. He texted her, "Would you like to go on a date with me sometime?" Two seconds later he received an enthusiastic reply: "Yes!" I can only assume that the reply was accompanied by a string of emojis.

After a month went by, I asked Mary Clare, "Have your two friends gone on their date yet?" "No," she said. I knew exactly why it hadn't happened yet because I've had the same issue going on my dates with my wife, Ginger. Experience has taught me that if I say to Ginger, "We should go see a movie sometime," and she says, "Yes, we should," we will never go to see a movie. If that's where the conversation ends, it won't happen. But if I say, "We should go see the new Marvel movie this Friday night at the movie theater at the mall," I can be *sure* that Ginger will say no, because she doesn't like Marvel movies. But you get the point. We only go when I'm specific. I have to suggest *when* we will see the movie—one she would want to see—and *where*. Deciding on those two things is the first step to enjoying popcorn in reclining seats and watching action on the big screen.

Deciding to pray is like making a date with God. Saying, "Hey, God, let's hang out sometime," is a good first step. But it sure helps to say, "Hey God, I'll meet you tomorrow afternoon, right after school; I'll be in the chair in the corner of my bedroom. I know you are with me all the time, but I want to find some time when I'm not doing anything else so I can give you my full attention."

I guarantee God will say, "See you there!"

conversation starters

- Talk about a time there was something you wanted to do but had trouble getting started. What got in the way?
- Think about your life and where you live. When and where would be good options for praying?
- Have a conversation about some places and times in the next few days that would be good for prayer. Decide on a place and time and try to keep your appointment.

part two

Ways to Pray

chapter thirteen

Ways to Pray with Scripture

Chewing on the Word

When children are young, we teach them the stories of the Bible—the greatest hits, you might say. We teach them about creation, about God saying, "Let there be light." We teach them about Noah and the flood—though we do leave out some of the more unsavory bits to focus on the animals, the olive branch, and the rainbow. We teach them about Jonah, because who doesn't love a story about a man swallowed and then regurgitated by a fish? And, of course, we teach them Jesus—birth, miracles, and parables, followed by betrayal, death, and ultimately resurrection. These are the stories we want them to know.

When I lead Bible studies with adults, I encounter a hunger for deeper understanding, a desire to know more. Many adults recognize that they never learned the stories between the few they learned as children. They sense the gaps in their knowledge, and they want to know more about what's on the pages bound between those faux leather covers.

For both children and adults, knowledge about the contents of the Bible is meaningful. However, while having an intellectual understanding is important, it also leaves something out: Scripture is not meant simply to inform us; it's meant to transform us as well.

Imagine that the scriptures are like a letter sent to us by someone who loves us very much, that it's personal communication.[10] When we receive such a letter, we savor it. We read it over and over, because, on some level, the letter is a vessel for that person's presence, bringing them closer to us. We read it slowly because we want to hear that person's voice speaking through the words on the page. Yes, the letter might convey interesting information, but its most important function is strengthening the relationship between us and the person who sent the letter.

When reading scripture, we are meant to hear the voice of the divine beloved. The words on the page are meant to convey the presence of God to us—a presence that transforms us through love.

The methods of prayer found in this section are aimed at helping kids transition from learning the stories *of* scripture—the head knowledge of the Bible—to encountering the transforming presence of God *through* scripture—the heart knowledge of God's word.

The first practice we'll cover has a Latin name: *lectio divina*, which simply means "sacred reading." Practiced in monasteries for centuries, *lectio divina* invites us to chew on scripture, savoring it like the rich feast that it is. This practice gives kids the opportunity to read a brief passage of scripture slowly, reflect on what they have read and what that has to do with their lives, and then respond to God in prayer. The practice moves kids from listening to God, who has the first word in this conversation, to speaking to God from the heart.

I recommend that kids begin with a vivid story from one of the Gospels. Stories with some dialogue and action, like the call of the first disciples (Mark 1:16-20), Jesus's healing of a man who was paralyzed (Mark 2:1-12), or the scene of Jesus's transfiguration (Luke 9:28-36) are wonderful options. Eventually, any passage of scripture can be used, but these Gospel stories are the most likely to keep the attention of young readers.

When practicing *lectio divina* with a group or when having kids share something about their experience, it's important for adults to remember not to correct what the kids say they are hearing from God. There are other settings better suited to helping them understand scripture; this is the time to be hospitable to their experience of God just as the practice is teaching them to be hospitable to God's word.

Kids will need a Bible or a print-out of a passage of scripture (it might be best to avoid using tablets and phones, as they provide infinite sources of distraction), along with something to write with and something to write on. The prompt below presents a *lectio divina* session using Mark 1:16-20 but can be easily adapted for other passages of scripture.

PRACTICE

- Find a comfortable place to sit—for instance, at a table where you can lay your Bible open in front of you. Get comfortable with your feet on the floor and your hands resting in your lap and then take a few deep breaths. Remind yourself that God is present and this is a special time to be open and available to God. Imagine that God is smiling at you, eager to spend this time with you. Scripture is like a letter God has written to you, and God is so glad you are going to spend this time reading it.
- Say a simple prayer, something like, "God, as I read these words, help me to slow down and listen. I want to hear you because I want to know you better and follow you more faithfully."
- Then turn in your Bible to Mark 1:16-20 or another passage of scripture you have selected to read. Read the passage slowly with an open mind and heart. There's no hurry. Imagine that you are eating one of your favorite foods and you want it to last; you want to savor every bite. Try not to anticipate what the passage is going to say, even if you've heard it before; read it as if for the first time.

Let it surprise you. As you read, simply notice anything that stands out or draws you in. It might be a word, a short phrase, or an image.

- Spend some time thinking about any word, phrase, or image from this passage that captured your attention. Why do you think it stuck out to you? What does it say to you about your life right now? What does it say to you about God? This is the part where you "chew on" the scripture and sit with whatever struck you. One way to do this is simply to repeat the word or phrase to yourself. Another is to think about a question that the passage has raised and consider it for a few moments. Whichever option you choose, spend a couple minutes reflecting on the passage.
- After you've spent some time reflecting on the passage (without rushing!), you can respond to God. This prayer is a conversation. God had the first word through scripture, and now you get to say something back. What does this passage of scripture make you want to talk to God about? Is it reminding you of something in your life that you need to share with God? Is there something puzzling or confusing? If you sense God saying something to you, do you want to tell God how that makes you feel? It can be anything you want!
- After you have responded by spending some time talking to God, take a few moments to rest in God's presence. Set your Bible aside and focus on your breathing. Take slow deep breaths to help settle your thoughts. As you do, you can repeat a short phrase like "I love you, God" or "I rest in you." This doesn't need to last a long time, maybe just a minute or two. This is a chance to be with God, enjoying the gift of God's presence.
- Finally, whisper a word of thanks to God for this time of prayer, and ask God to help you keep this passage of scripture in mind as you go about the rest of your activities for the day.

VARIATIONS

- You can do this with a group. Have someone read the passage aloud and share the instructions, "Spend a couple of minutes reflecting on a word, phrase, or image that stuck out to you." After a couple of minutes, they should invite participants to share the word or phrase (nothing else). Then, the leader reads the passage aloud again. This time they should say, "Now spend some time silently talking to God about how this passage of scripture touched you." After a couple of minutes, the leader can close with a simple prayer of thanks.
- Start a prayer journal and keep a record of the different passages you have used for this practice. For each one, note one word that summarizes or captures your experience of the practice. If you sensed that God was leading you through this activity, make a note of how.
- Use the same passage for a few days in a row. Pay attention to how the experience changes each day. Do you notice different aspects of the passage? Do different things stick out to you?

Mary Clare says . . .

When I have read scripture in the past, I have found it difficult, usually because I don't *understand* it. I mean, scripture is definitely confusing, and so, as someone who has lots of questions and wants to understand everything, reading scripture is difficult because I can't always get the answers I want.

Recently, I went to a youth Bible study at my church, and we talked through a passage in Matthew about building your life on faith and on God by following the teachings of Jesus. It was a lovely time, but I walked out feeling like I had no idea how to do that. I was sure of my faith and sure of God, but it was challenging to know how to build my life on that when I had never really read the Bible with "success." How was I supposed to know what to do when I didn't know the instructions?

On the way home from Bible study, I told my mom I wanted to start reading the Bible. I wanted to work my way through it so I could grow in my faith. The next morning, I woke up twenty minutes earlier than usual, sat at my desk with a steamy cup of coffee (yes, my parents let me drink coffee), and read the first chapter of Matthew. But instead of trying to understand it or have all my questions answered, I did what this prayer practice suggests: I tried to listen to how this passage was speaking to me in the moment.

The beginning of that chapter is all about Jesus's ancestors, and the passage names him as a son of David and a son of Abraham. This didn't make sense right away, because wasn't Jesus's "dad" Joseph? Or technically, isn't his father God? But instead of trying to find answers to those questions, I let the words of the scripture sink in. If Jesus can be titled son of Abraham and son of David, even though they lived hundreds of years before him, then I am surely a daughter of God even though God was there at the beginning of time—a very, very long time before me!

I wrote this thought down in my journal, along with a quick prayer for the day, and got ready for school.

Imagine It, Enter It

It's been a long time since I've watched *Dora the Explorer*, but there's something about that show, and so many other programs for children, that's hard to forget—the way Dora looks right at the camera and speaks directly with the kids watching as if they are part of the adventure. In theater this technique is called "breaking the fourth wall," because it ignores the imaginary wall between stage and audience and invites the spectators right into the scene.

When we read scripture prayerfully, we can use our imaginations to do the same thing. We can step right into the story and imagine we are there. What do we notice from this new perspective? How do we feel as we enter the scene? How does this vantage point change how we understand what's going on in the story or what's going on in ourselves?

This imaginative approach to praying with scripture was popularized by St. Ignatius of Loyola, the sixteenth-century Spanish founder of a religious order called the Jesuits. When explaining this type of prayer, Ignatius said that the first step was to use your imagination to picture the scene and ask yourself, "What do you see, feel, and hear?" If you are reading the story about the disciples in a boat when a storm arises, you might imagine the waves, hear the wind, and see the looks of fear on the disciples' faces.

Once you have composed the scene in your mind, then you step into it—placing yourself right in the story. In the example we used in "Chewing on the Word," you might imagine that you are *in* the boat with the disciples. What do you feel as you place yourself in the tossed and battered boat? Can you sense the fear in yourself? Can you imagine the feeling of the water spraying on your face? Are you frozen, watching the others run about frantically, or do you get to work, heaving water from the boat?

The final step, according to Ignatius, involves an imagined conversation with Jesus (or another character in the story, but for kids it might be best to stick with Jesus). Given your imagined experience in the story, what do you want to say to Jesus? What do you want to ask him? In this example, you might say something like, "Jesus, I've been noticing lately that my life feels like a boat battered by the waves—help me to see and trust you in the midst of this." And then, you can spend a few moments imagining what Jesus might say to you in reply. (A good guess is that he would say something he frequently says to the disciples: "Do not be afraid.")

Learning to pray this way was difficult for me. I first started practicing this type of prayer as an adult, and I was uncomfortable using my imagination in this way. I wasn't sure I could trust it. But then I remembered that the point of prayer is to trust Jesus. I suspect most kids will have no problem engaging their imagination in prayer. In fact, some of them might find themselves excitedly thinking, "Why didn't someone teach me this sooner?"

I suggest beginning with short passages from the Gospels. In the example that follows, I'll be using the story of Bartimaeus from Mark 10:46-52. Once both adults and kids get familiar with this practice, the script can be adjusted to accommodate almost any Gospel story.

THE PRACTICE

- As you begin, find Mark 10:46-52 in your Bible. Put a bookmark in the passage and then set it aside. Take two or three slow, deep breaths, then imagine that God is looking at you with delight, so happy that you have chosen to spend this time in God's presence. Take a few moments to enjoy the thought of God smiling at you.
- Now whisper a prayer to God as you get ready to read the passage of scripture. You can say this prayer silently or out loud. Pray something like, "God, as I read this story about your son, Jesus, help me to enter the story so I can know, love, and follow you better each day. Thank you for your love in my life."
- Slowly read the passage to get a feeling for the whole story (or have someone else read it to you). When you get to the end, go back to the beginning and read it again. This time use your imagination to picture the story, like you are watching a play or a movie. There's no right way to do this, and you don't have to make it look a certain way in your mind. When the story mentions a city (like Jericho), you can imagine any version of a town or a city. Can you

picture the large crowd that's with Jesus? What do the people look like? What are they wearing? Can you imagine the sound of Bartimaeus's voice as he shouts to Jesus? Imagine what he looks like when he throws off his cloak and runs to Jesus. Just read the story slowly and free your imagination to picture the scene.

- Now read the story a third time—still slowly—and put yourself *in* the story. This might feel awkward but let your imagination run free. Where do you see yourself? Are you standing in the crowd watching? Are you one of the disciples who hushes Bartimaeus? Are you sitting on the ground next to Bartimaeus? Now that you are in the scene, how do you feel as the story happens? How do you feel when you hear Bartimaeus shout out or when the disciples shush him? How do you feel when Jesus has the disciples call him over? Excited? Nervous? Are you surprised that Jesus asks, "What do you want me to do for you?" How do you feel when you see that Bartimaeus has regained his sight? Take all the time you want to explore this story from the inside using your imagination. Remember to keep paying attention to yourself—what you are feeling, thinking, and noticing.
- Finally, imagine that you remain in this story after everything you've watched. As it settles down, start a conversation with Jesus. What do you want to ask him? What's the first thing you would say? Imagine him asking you, "What do you want me to do for *you*?" What would you say? How do you think Jesus would respond to you? Spend some time sharing your thoughts or questions with Jesus about this story and what it has to do with *your* life.
- When you are done, offer a prayer to God expressing thanks for the gift of this time to spend in God's presence as a friend, and especially for the wonderful gift of your imagination.

VARIATIONS

- You can use this practice with a group. A leader reads the story aloud first, inviting the others to picture the scene, then reads it again, inviting them to enter it with their imaginations. The leader can suggest prompts for imagining as I have above. Finally, the leader gives those participating time to imagine a conversation with Jesus. Afterward, participants can share something they noticed while imagining the story or something they talked with Jesus about.
- Do this prayer practice a few times using the same story. Each time, imagine entering the story from a different perspective and notice what difference this makes to how you perceive it. In the passage used above, the first time you might imagine that you are part of the crowd, just watching, but the second time you might imagine you are Bartimaeus—*that* would change things!
- Keep a record of each time you do this practice. Write down the scripture passage and next to it write one word summarizing your experience of praying with that passage.

Draw Your Prayer

Many adults may feel like we have graduated from the need to use crayons, colored pencils, and markers to help us pray, so it might be that the kids, with their imaginations still uninhibited, will guide *us* into rediscovering this creative way of prayer. You don't need to be an artist to draw your way into communion with God.

While some kids will be drawn to a prayer practice that invites them to use their imaginations, picturing in their minds a scene from scripture and then imagining themselves within it (see, "Picture It, Enter It"), others will benefit from getting these images out of their heads and onto paper. They may connect with God easier through the practice of moving a marker across the page and watching their prayer come to life in color before their eyes. This way of praying with scripture gives kids (and daring adults) a green light to do just that.

All kids need is paper and markers, colored pencils, or crayons—that, and the reminder that there are no rules here, no right way to draw a scene from scripture or to put the deepest prayer of their heart into pictures.

As with "Picture It, Enter It," it will be most helpful to use a story from the Gospels to try out this prayer practice. Since these stories are narratives, they have characters and scenes that are easier to imagine and draw. I suggest beginning with the call of the first disciples in the Gospel of Mark (Mark 1:16-20). There are other passages that can work equally well: Jesus's healing of a man who was paralyzed (Mark 2:1-12); the shepherds going to see the baby Jesus (Luke 2:8-20); and the resurrection of Jesus (John 20:1-10 and 11-18).

Something to remember: When engaging kids in conversation about what they draw, stay curious, letting them take the lead. Since this isn't an art contest, don't compliment them or praise them for their drawing. Rather, lead them into conversation with open questions that let the kids explore what they have drawn, questions like, "Will you tell me something about your drawing?" "What does your drawing mean to you?" or "What does your drawing say about God?" Of course, it's fine not to have conversation at all, and older kids can do this without a grown-up around.

THE PRACTICE

- Gather what you need—a Bible, blank paper, and some markers, crayons, or colored pencils—and settle into a comfortable place to pray like a desk or a kitchen table. Then, spend a few moments sitting still and imagining that God is smiling on you, so pleased that you want to spend this time with God. Take some time to enjoy that thought. Next, whisper a short prayer, something like,

"God, it's good to be with you, and I'm especially excited to pray with art supplies! Guide me as I read your word and use drawing to express my prayer to you." Use your own words; make the prayer your own.

- Open to the selected passage of scripture, ideally a story from one of the Gospels, and read it. Pay attention to what's going on: Who is in the scene? Where are they? What are they doing? How are they interacting with Jesus?
- Then, draw! Once you've read the story, begin to draw whatever comes into your mind. An easy way to begin is to simply start drawing a part of the scene that captured your attention—maybe it's an object that's in the story, or a particularly interesting character, or the whole scene. There's no right way to do this.
- It's possible that something else came to mind as you read, like a memory or a feeling. You can also choose to draw that. If you are drawing an emotion or feeling, you might only want to use colors or shapes to get the feeling onto paper. Did the story feel joyful to you? Then, perhaps draw a sun. Did it make you feel sad? If so, you might want to draw gray clouds and rain. It's up to you—this is *your* prayer.
- Keep drawing for as long as you like—this isn't a race. You can draw with as much or as little detail as you please. If your mind starts to wander or if you get distracted, you can read the passage of scripture again and then return to drawing.
- When you feel like you are finished, take a look at what you drew and ask yourself: What does my picture make me think God was trying to say to me? What does my picture make me think I was trying to say to God? Is there anything that surprises me about what I drew? Anything that makes me happy?
- Finish by talking with God about what you drew and thanking God for God's friendship and love. Thank God especially for the

gift of creativity and art that can help us grow in our relationship with God, even when we don't know what to say.

VARIATIONS

- You can practice this way of prayer with others. A leader can read the passage and give time for others to draw. At the end, they can be invited to share with this simple prompt: "Show us your drawing and tell us something in your picture that is meaningful to you or makes you think of God."
- After using this prayer practice, hang the drawing in a place where you will see it often. When you see it, allow it to remind you of the scripture passage you read and what you sensed God saying to you or what you wanted to say to God.
- Do this practice several times with the same passage of scripture and keep your drawings in a folder. After completing about five to seven drawings, spend some time looking through them. Do you notice any similarities? Did you draw wildly different things on different days? Can you sense what these drawings, over time, might have been trying to say to God?

In Your Own Words

Martin Luther, the sixteenth-century Protestant reformer, said of the book of Psalms: "In it is comprehended most beautifully and briefly everything that is in the entire Bible."[11] He knew that the psalms—those 150 poems and prayers smack in the middle of the Bible—are a treasure and that there are more gifts waiting to be unwrapped in this book of the Bible than we can number.

Here's one of those gifts: The psalms tutor us in prayer. They are guides that can help us express praise to God, name disappointment, cry out to God in anger, and snuggle up to God in comfort. As tutors, they teach us something we are never too young or too old to learn: Nothing is off limits in prayer. There is no emotion too deep (see "Big Feelings") or situation too distressing for God to judge out of bounds for prayer. There's *nothing* we can't take to God.

I have a practice of praying through the psalms, reading a few each morning and each evening, so that I read all 150 every two months. This practice is valuable as the words and moods of the psalms seep into my bones and become part of me. Repeating the words of the psalms is one way these poems can teach us.

But we can also allow the psalms to be models and inspirations for our own prayer. I remember one particular afternoon in 2009 when life's burdens seemed excruciatingly heavy, not least because my eighty-eight-year-old father was near death. I retreated to my study, sat down, and turned to Psalm 130, a psalm that cries to God from a place of despair, but also one that expresses hope in God's deliverance. After reading the psalm, I opened my journal and began writing. Using the psalm as a prompt, I penned my own prayer, putting the sentiments of the psalm into my own words, words relevant to my situation. As I did this, tears tumbled down my cheeks and dotted the pages of my journal.

Kids can do this too. Not every psalm will speak to the situations of young people, but kids also know joy as well as sadness, hope as well as pain, gladness as well as fear, and if it's true that God wants to be their friend (it is), then learning to bring their whole selves to God can strengthen that friendship and grow their trust in God's steadfast love.

It might be useful to begin with a psalm of praise (like Psalm 100). Eventually kids can move to psalms of comfort (like Psalm 23), or even psalms of longing (like Psalms 42 or 63) and other psalms that voice distress (like Psalm 130). Kids should be reminded that there is no right way to do this and that verses they don't understand or that don't connect with them can simply be skipped. Also, this isn't a writing contest—so they shouldn't worry if it's *good*. This is prayer.

THE PRACTICE

- After choosing a psalm, settle into a comfortable place with a Bible, some paper, and something to write with. Breathe in and out deeply a couple of times, then take a few moments to imagine that God is looking at you and smiling. There's no hurry, so rest, knowing that God loves you so much. Then whisper a prayer to God, thanking God for these quiet moments to spend in God's presence.
- Read the psalm you have chosen. Pay attention to what sticks out to you. Notice if anything connects with you or feels meaningful to you. Feel free to ignore verses that don't make any sense to you or that seem too strange. Instead, pay attention to a verse or two that express something you are feeling or hoping for. Reread these verses a couple of times.
- Now it's time to write. Think about how you would put the psalm into your own words. If the psalm is short, like Psalm 100, you can rewrite the whole thing. If it is longer, or there are sections of the psalm that don't make sense to you, pick the verses that caught your attention or seemed meaningful to you. Remember, you are writing this as a prayer to God, and it is *your* prayer—there is no right way to do this. If you only use five words, that's fine; if it takes you five hundred, that's fine too. No one is going to grade what you have written! It's natural for this to feel a little awkward the first few times. The key is to simply relax and let go. Write the words that come to you.
- You might find at first that you are going verse by verse, rewriting the psalm in your own words. Eventually though, you may stop

looking at the words in your Bible and just continue writing to God about whatever is on your heart or mind. This is perfectly fine. It's good actually! You are letting the psalm in the Bible help you get your own prayer started, and that's the whole point.

- When you feel like you are done, read aloud to God what you have written. Let the words on paper come to life on your lips.

VARIATIONS

- You can do this prayer practice with a group. All the members of the group should use the same psalm. A leader can read the psalm out loud to the group, but each participant should have a copy of the psalm in front of them. At the end of the practice, members of the group can be invited to share their prayers with one another, remembering that this is not a contest.
- Try doing this practice about once a week using different psalms. Get a special notebook or journal for your writing and periodically go back and review the prayers you have written. Soon you will have a small collection of your own prayers.
- You can also do this without writing. Just read the psalm and *say* a prayer to God inspired by the psalm. Put the psalm into your own words without writing anything down.

chapter fourteen

Ways to Pray That Are Quiet

Sacred Word, Sacred Breath

In the late fourth and early fifth centuries, there was a monk named John Cassian. Cassian traveled to Palestine and Egypt to interview other monks about prayer and living a life of faith. He learned their secrets of prayer and perseverance and how these monks, living in harsh landscapes, practiced relying on God in all things. His writings had a significant impact on the development of Christian spirituality in the West. One wise monk told him that all you need is to cling to one short prayer, one verse of scripture, and have it on your heart and in your mouth at all times. He said this is especially true when you need to cry out to God and suggested using a verse of a psalm: "Be pleased, O God, to deliver me. O LORD, make haste to help me!" (Psalm 70:1).[12]

This advice marks an early example of the use of a sacred word or phrase in prayer, and as this kind of prayer developed it took many forms. We are used to thinking of using a mantra as a practice of Eastern religions, but Christians have used prayer words or phrases—essentially mantras—for centuries to help them find stillness in their minds and hearts and center their lives on the love of God.

This style of prayer remains accessible today, and it is one that kids of all ages can easily learn. It's simple, but powerful. It involves repeating a prayer word or phrase in the mind while timing the repetition of the word with the flow of one's breath. Throughout history, the most common phrase used has been a version of what's called the Jesus Prayer: "Lord Jesus Christ, Son of God, have mercy on me, a sinner." But other phrases work just as well: "Be still and know that I am God," "I trust in You," "I love You." Even a single word can be used: "Jesus," "Abba," "Love," "Peace"—any word or phrase that symbolizes the desire of the one praying to dwell in the presence and compassion of God.

This form of prayer can become a refuge from the myriad thoughts that constantly haunt our minds and scream for our attention. What kid doesn't know the pressure of these insistent, seductive voices: *You aren't good enough! You aren't pretty enough! You aren't popular enough!* I can't think of a prayer practice more relevant to the challenges of being a kid today than one that helps kids release these sticky thoughts from their attention so that they can return their hearts and minds to an inner sanctuary in which they dwell securely in God's love, acceptance, and peace.

The following example of a prayer practice is one that I have written about elsewhere for adults, and it's a version of a very old Christian way of praying.[13]

THE PRACTICE

- Find a comfortable place to sit or lie down. When you feel settled, spend a few moments remembering how much God loves you. Imagine how delighted God is that you have chosen to take some time to spend in God's presence. Simply being with God is bringing a big, dimply smile to God's face! Allow yourself to feel God smiling at you.

- Now choose a word or phrase that helps you think about God's love. I recommend "Your love never fails," "Thank you for your love," or "I love you." You can also choose a single word like "Love," "Peace," or the name "Jesus."
- Begin to repeat this word or phrase to yourself silently. Time the repetition of the word with your breathing. If your phrase is, "Your love never fails," say "Your love" while you are breathing in and "never fails" while you are breathing out. If you have chosen a single word like "Peace," say the word to yourself both while you are breathing in and breathing out. Try to focus your attention on the word as you repeat it.
- Be patient, because after a few seconds, you might realize that you are no longer repeating the word or paying attention to it. Instead, you are thinking about other things like homework you have to do, an argument you had with a friend, or how delicious your lunch was yesterday—you might start thinking about anything!
- When this happens—when you notice that you have become lost in other thoughts—don't despair. It's good that you have recognized this. All you have to do is start silently to say the word again, time it with your breath, and give it your attention. This will happen over and over again, and it's nothing to worry about. Our minds are made to think! But right now, since you want to be still in God's presence, when you find yourself thinking about things, simply notice that it's happening and then start repeating the word again, giving it your attention.
- Sometimes people find this very relaxing after a few minutes; sometimes people get frustrated that they keep getting distracted. Either is fine. What really matters is that you have chosen to spend time intentionally being in God's presence. It doesn't have to feel a certain way. One day your mind is busy, another day it's calm. It

changes all the time. But God's love for you never does, and God enjoys when you take a few moments to spend with God.

- After a few minutes of praying this way, you can end by whispering a prayer to God, something like, "God here I am, and here you are. I'm glad to have this time to rest in your presence."

VARIATIONS

- Try this practice with others, with a grown-up or perhaps your friends. Sit in a circle and set a timer for a certain length of time (two minutes, ten minutes, it doesn't matter). Sit in the silence together. When the timer goes off, end by saying the Lord's Prayer together. You might want to share your prayer words or phrases with each other and say why the word or phrase is meaningful for you.
- This practice is portable. It can be done while walking, sitting bored in the back seat of the car, or while bumping along on a school bus. Try it anywhere!
- Do this practice for two minutes a day, at the same time, for one week. At the end of the week, think about the difference it made to spend this time with God each day in this way. If you keep a journal, write your thoughts in the journal. Praying like this can become a simple habit you can do every day, like brushing teeth or eating breakfast.

Morning Offering

Morning is a special time to pray. Those first minutes when we shake off the lethargy of sleep, watch our dreams slink away, and open our hearts to the possibilities inherent in a new day. What will we and God paint together on this fresh canvas?

The Bible depicts Jesus waking early on several occasions to spend time alone with God (see Mark 2:35 for instance). Now, this practice doesn't suggest anyone should wake up earlier than usual, especially kids, who need their sleep. But it does allow kids to take those first holy minutes of the day and use them to turn their attention to God before anything else.

This practice can be particularly important considering what many of us, even kids, do first thing in the morning—reach for our phones. The light of the screen becomes the first light we see. It dilates our pupils as we hungrily investigate what we missed while we were asleep—social media updates, group texts, email messages, and, for adults, news and weather forecasts. That fleeting sense of the almost limitless possibilities of the day—along with the hope of staying awake to God—evaporates.

But it doesn't have to be that way. Those first moments of the morning can be—before anything else—a time to receive the gift of a new day and offer that day—with all our plans, worries, and hopes—to God.

Of course, the kids in our lives begin their days with their own plans—to attend swim practice, head to school, meet a friend for a walk. Yet, as adults, we know the truth behind the old joke: "How do you make God laugh? Make a plan." Living a life with God involves a balance between sticking to our own plans and knowing that when they don't go as we would like (a kid forgets a lunchbox and misses a field trip, an illness causes a kid to cancel a birthday party, bad weather postpones a sporting event), God is still with us and our lives still belong to God. New possibilities for receiving and showing God's love open at each moment, even when things don't go as planned—an important lesson for a young person to learn in God's company.

This prayer practice invites kids to open their spirits to God first thing in the morning and offer the gift of their day to God, acknowledging that, even when the day doesn't go as planned, it—and they—still belong to God.

THE PRACTICE

- After you wake, before doing anything else, sit on the edge of the bed and enjoy the thought that God is looking at you with love and smiling on you. God loves that you are rested and awake, and God is eager to share this new day with you. Sit in the quiet for as long as you like and soak in the fact that God delights in you.
- Take three or four slow, deep breaths, in and out through your nose, as a way of settling into this moment. If your thoughts are already zooming off in a thousand different directions, or if you are already worried about something else the day might bring, then pay attention to your breath—the sound of it at the tip of your nose and the rise and fall of your belly—and let the racing thoughts drift away.
- Now place your hands together in your lap in the shape of a bowl, like a large cereal bowl sitting on your lap. Think about what you have going on today. Whenever you think of something, imagine that you are putting it in the bowl made by your hands, slowly filling the bowl with your day. Do you have a test at school that you're anxious about? Put it in the bowl. Is there a field trip you are looking forward to? Put it in the bowl. Let your mind roam through the upcoming day and place whatever you notice in the bowl. Doing this is like placing your life in the bowl.
- After you have placed all your worries, hopes, and plans into the bowl you've made with your hands, slowly lift your hands, keeping them in the shape of a bowl (we don't want anything to leak out!) until they are higher than your head, as if you are lifting them to God. As you do this, say a short prayer to God, either silently or out loud, something like, "God, here is my day—my hopes, worries, and plans—and I offer it to you in love. I don't really know what's going to happen today, and I don't have control

over very much. Help me notice you in my day, help me love others, and when things don't go according to plan, help me offer my frustration to you as well, remembering that you always hold me in love." You can also simply raise your day to God, without words or thoughts, knowing that you are offering it to the God who loves all that you are.

- Finally, lower your hands, take three or four more slow breaths, and move on with your day.

VARIATIONS

- My favorite prayer for the morning goes like this:

  > New every morning is your love, great God of light, and all day long you are working for good in the world. Stir up in us desire to serve you, to live peacefully with our neighbors and all your creation, and to devote each day to your Son, our Savior Jesus Christ. Amen.[14]

  Try memorizing this prayer and saying it at the end of this practice as a closing prayer.

- Use this prayer practice at any time of the day including as a midday prayer or in the middle of a time when things aren't going as planned. At any time, you can pause, fill the bowl of your hands with whatever is going on, and lift it to God.
- It's hard to do this one with others, but if others in your family are using this practice, it can be something to talk about. Someone can ask, "What did you put into the bowl of your hands this morning and offer to God?" You can tell them and ask them the same question in return. If your youth group or Sunday school class is doing this together, simply have conversation about how using this prayer practice went during the week.

Mary Clare says . . .

Honestly, the first thing I do every morning before school is scroll on my phone to let the vibrant glow wake up my tired brain since it's dark out and hard for me to get myself up so early. I know it's not the healthiest way to wake up and usually results in a mini-headache, but I do it anyway. This prayer practice of a morning offering challenges that habit, so I decided to try it a few days before my first day of school, and I started waking up before 6:30 every day to get used to it.

The first day my alarm woke me up, but after I turned off the alarm, I put the phone down and sat up. I didn't move to the edge of my bed or make my bed then do it or get dressed first—I stayed right where I'd been sleeping, still under my blankets, comfy, warm, and surprisingly not sleepy because I was already paying attention to God. I took a few deep breaths and set my attention upon God. I cupped my hands in my lap and began to comb through the day ahead, putting each thing in the cup.

I'm busy in the summers, especially in the days before school starts. I have tennis matches, marching band rehearsals, last-minute visits to the pool before it closes for the year, shopping trips for back-to-school items, and plenty of time spent hanging out with friends to savor those last days of summer. That first day, I had some combination of all of those things coming up, and I was decently stressed. But I put each event of the day in my hands one by one, raised them up to God, and simply said, "Be with me today as I live, guide me towards love and care, and let me be at peace with whatever happens."

And it was a perfect way to start my day. No mindless scrolling, no toxic phone lights, no headaches. Just me, my day, and God.

The hardest thing about this exercise wasn't trying to stay awake or keeping my mind from wandering, it was trying to steer away from asking God for everything to go the way I wanted it to go. I knew it wouldn't, and instead I needed to ask God to help me be flexible with whatever happens.

On the third day I did this practice, the morning before school started, I was sick. I wanted *so badly* to get better, for my fever to go down, and to be able to go to school on the first day in my perfectly planned back-to-school outfit wearing my new backpack that was organized for my classes and be with all my friends. I knew I was prone to missing things because I get fevers easily, and I was tempted to just ask God, "*Please*, I know I've missed other things from being sick and I'm used to it, but *please* God, just let me do this one thing." I almost asked.

But it was far more important for me to put this worry in my cup, lift it to God, and say, "God, I'm sick, and that sucks. If I miss school tomorrow, help me to be okay with it and know that you are still with me." And that changed my mindset for the rest of the day.

Ultimately, I missed the first day, but I took it as a blessing to get all the last things done—clean my room, make a to-do list, have more time to finish the schoolwork my teachers sent me. I even got to eat breakfast with my dad outside on the back porch, bask in the sun, and enjoy one more day of summer. Although things didn't go as I wanted, I was able to be at peace with the disruption. And I can thank the time I was able to spend with God first thing in the morning for that.

Looking Back, Looking for God

Sometimes, at the end of the day, it's nice to look back on the day and ask, "Where did I see God today?" or "Where did God seem absent today?" This practice of prayer invites kids to do just that, honing their attentiveness to God in the process.

But what does it mean to "look for God"? We are not going to see God like we might see a squirrel running across the yard. But we can "see" God in the goodness or kindness of others or in our own actions. We can also feel God when we feel a sense of connection or belonging. God is present when we respond to an opportunity to show love or when we find ourselves simply being ourselves—and it feels *right.* Kids can see God in these ways, too.

At other times, we ignore God, for instance, when we reject goodness in others or ourselves, or when we recognize an opportunity to show love but ignore it. On occasion, it can feel like God is far away or absent, like when we see people acting cruelly, or when we feel disconnected and lonely. God isn't *actually* absent, but in those moments it can feel that way. Being able to notice these moments without being afraid or ashamed of them is so important as children learn to trust God. There's nothing *wrong* when they feel this way.

This way of prayer is sometimes called an *examen*. I'm reluctant to use that word because it has "exam" in it, which sounds like a test, and what kid wants prayer to feel like a test? When you are leading kids through an *examen*, you are really just helping them take *a careful look*. This quiet way to pray helps kids to look at their lives with intention and care in the hope that their capacity to pay attention and be aware of God's goodness in each moment will grow. When someone prays this way, consistently and over time, they get better at noticing God and saying "Yes!" in the moment when divine love calls to them.

While this method of prayer can be used at any time, most people do it at the end of the day to look back at how God has been present.

THE PRACTICE

- Find a comfortable, quiet place to pray—someplace where you won't be distracted. Take a few deep breaths to help you clear your mind. Imagine God smiling at you and simply rest for a few moments in that feeling of being loved. God delights in you, so enjoy it!

- Pray something like, "God, I'm taking this time to pray because I want to recognize your presence and love in my life. Give me the grace to see what I need to see. Open my mind and heart to your presence and love."
- Then let your mind recall your day. What did you do today? Where did you go? Who did you see? Simply let your mind roam through the day for a little while and pay attention to what seems most significant. Were there any big moments? Any hard ones? Do this for a couple of minutes.
- Now look through your day and notice any times when you felt love, peace, or joy. Look for times you felt connection or belonging. Don't rush through these! What was going on in these moments? Try to remember the feelings and savor those moments. Silently give God thanks for touching your life with these gifts of grace.
- Look through your day again and notice any times when you felt angry, mean, empty, or lost. Look for times when you felt disconnected or lonely. Don't rush, even though these might not be pleasant feelings. What was going on in these moments? Is there anything you need to say "I'm sorry" for? In the silence, ask God to help you remember God's love and grace even in times when things feel hard.
- Finally, reflect on what you noticed in this time of prayer. What is any of this telling you about how God is working in your life? How do you hope tomorrow will be different? Say a silent prayer, asking God to help you be aware of God's love tomorrow, so that you can enjoy God's love and show God's love to those around you. Thank God for being present and guiding you in this time of prayer.

VARIATIONS

- Instead of doing this practice only in your mind, write down what you notice in a journal. Alternatively, when the prayer practice is finished, write down *one word* or draw a simple picture that captures what this time of prayer has meant to you.
- For a shorter version, just ask two questions to help you look at your day: "When did I notice and respond to love in my life today?" and "When did I ignore or reject love in my life today?"
- You can use this practice with a group of friends or with the whole family by having someone walk through the prayer practice slowly, remembering to pause and provide time for reflection. Then, at the end, each person can share briefly one thing they noticed during the time of prayer that seemed particularly meaningful or important.

Bathed in Light

Some of the most challenging questions kids (and adults) have about prayer involve praying for others. How do we know what to pray for? How specific should we be? If a friend broke her arm, how do I pray for her? Do I ask God to give her patience, ease her pain, heal her overnight—or all three? What does it mean about God when I ask for these things and they don't seem to happen? Has God ignored me? Has God said no? These questions arise from a type of prayer known as intercession—praying to God on behalf of others. As adults, we sometimes simply ignore these insistent questions, but curious kids won't let them go.

I've struggled with these questions myself. For a long time, intercession was one of the hardest types of prayer for me because it presented so many puzzles. Eventually, in Marjorie Thompson's book *Soul Feast*, I discovered a way of praying for others that doesn't involve telling God what God should do but uses the imagination to hold the one we are praying for in God's healing light.[15] This quiet way of prayer is not necessarily about talking to God, but about bringing someone into God's presence and trusting God's goodness to know what to do.

Think about the story found in the Gospel of Mark where four friends carry someone they love to Jesus. They climb onto the top of a house, dig through the roof, and lower their paralyzed friend in front of Jesus. But then they leave it there, trusting that their friend is in Jesus's presence and Jesus will know what to do and will act with wisdom and compassion (Mark 2:1-12). This form of prayer does the same. It encourages us to use our imagination to bring the people we are praying for into God's presence, fully trusting God's healing, whole-making grace.

Kids worry about friends and family members. At times, my kids have witnessed my own challenges and struggles. For instance, they've seen me hobbling around with a cane when my arthritis flares up and once they saw me consumed by pain in my torso, writhing on the couch with what turned out to be an angry gallbladder. I have seen the fear, worry, and concern in their eyes. By teaching kids this prayer practice, we are giving them a tool—something they can use to deal with the things they are carrying around. They can carry someone they know and love, someone who is suffering or facing a challenge to God by holding them in God's presence.

Kids can feel frozen when they see others hurting, but when they bless their friends and those they love with this prayer, they are doing something meaningful. Carrying their friend to God, even if they don't know what their friend needs, is a good thing. I trust that kids will find this way of prayer liberating and empowering, just as I did.

The description of the practice that follows is inspired by what I learned from Marjorie Thompson's book *Soul Feast.*

THE PRACTICE

- Find a comfortable place to sit or stand for a few minutes and begin to imagine God smiling at you. You may be feeling worried about someone you care about but know that God is looking compassionately at you. Can you imagine how glad God feels to see that you care so much about this person? Stay here for a few moments, enjoying the thought of how much God loves you.
- Now picture someone you care about who is facing some kind of challenge. This could be a friend who is sick, a family member who is stressed and worried, or a teacher who is going through a tough time. Picture them as clearly as you can and imagine them feeling relaxed, peaceful, and at ease. If this is a challenge, get a photo of the person you are praying for and look at the photo to help you focus on them. For a few moments, see this person in your imagination and let yourself feel love and compassion for them.
- Then begin to imagine God's grace—God's own love and compassion—washing over them. You can imagine this any way you like. Maybe, in your imagination, it looks like a rain shower, but instead of water, it's falling pearls of light. Or maybe it's more like a stream of watery light covering them in its glow. Whatever way you imagine it, just watch in your mind as this healing flow of light comes from God and embraces the person you are praying for. Can you see how the light is flowing over them and surrounding them? This is the light of God's grace, love, peace, and compassion. You don't need to say anything to God or speak any words. God knows what this person needs. You are simply holding this person in the light of God's love, and that is enough. Do this for as long as you like.

- When you are finished, you can whisper a prayer, something like, "Thank you God for your love. Thank you for looking after this person and for caring so much for me." You can also simply sit in silence for a few minutes, letting your own presence be an expression of love and gratitude to God.

VARIATIONS

- You can do this practice with small group by praying for the same person at the same time, or each person in the group can choose a different person. Someone can remind them of the practice or guide them through it together. A Sunday school class, youth group, or group of friends can do this together.
- Try using this practice every day for a week, praying for the same person, someone you see regularly. Pay attention to that person throughout the week and notice your own feelings: How do you feel about that person after praying for them on a regular basis? Sometimes, when we pray for someone, we discover that our own compassion for them grows.
- Keep a list of the people you are praying for and let this practice of prayer become a regular part of your life. You might find that God has given you a gift or passion for praying for others, and this might be a way you can serve God and others throughout your life.

chapter fifteen

Ways to Pray with Your Body

Body Prayer

We know that we can pray with words, and we know that we can form prayers of thanksgiving and petition with our thoughts. Some of us might have grown up hearing our parents tell us: "Don't forget to say your prayers before bed." We might tell our children the same. All of those prayers are good, and they are valuable.

However, along with wordy, thought-filled prayers, I also want this book to encourage kids (and the adults who love them) to discover that simply *being* can also be a kind of prayer as we offer our very existence to God. That means, along with our minds and our mouths, our *bodies* can pray too. For kids, who tend to feel more ease and comfort expressing themselves with their bodies than adults—we adults can so easily get trapped in our own heads—praying with their bodies can feel natural and liberating. Body prayer is also deeply Christian. When we call Jesus "Emmanuel," which means "God with us," we are celebrating the fact that Jesus—God's Son—took on our flesh and offered his whole life to God as a kind of prayer. Jesus himself is God's body prayer.

This practice of body prayer consists of a series of gestures that allows kids to use their bodies to express their intention to *receive* the gifts of God's love, grace, and goodness; to show their *gratitude* for those gifts; to affirm their desire to live lives that *share* those gifts with others; and to *praise* God for who God is—a God of love, grace, and goodness. What follows suggests particular gestures that any kid can follow. Eventually, kids may want to improvise their own meaningful gestures, ones that help them connect more deeply with the concepts of receiving, giving thanks, sharing, and praising.

THE PRACTICE

- Stand and become aware of your body. Let yourself feel relaxed as you do, and simply notice how your body is feeling, without feeling the need to change anything. Be—just as you are. Imagine God is smiling on you—on your whole self, and especially on your physical body that God made and loves. This body is such a miracle! You might want to say out loud, "Thank you God for this body of mine!"
- Now bring to mind the thought of *receiving* something, like a gift. Slowly stretch out your arms with your palms up and imagine that you are receiving the abundance of God's love, because you are. Stretch out your hands like you might if you were outside in the rain and wanted to feel the raindrops splashing on your palms. Imagine that God's love, grace, and goodness are raining down on you and you want to catch it all. Then slowly bring your hands together and pull them to your chest, as if you are holding a delicate butterfly near to your chest to keep it safe, to cherish it. Imagine that you are drawing the gifts of love, grace, and goodness—the gifts that God is pouring out on you—close to your heart and cherishing them. You can repeat this gesture several times. Say, "God, I receive and cherish your love," as you repeat the gesture.

- The last time you practice this receiving gesture, bring your palms together in a praying motion, with your fingers pointing up, and slowly raise your hands, pressed gently together, in front of your face. Hold them there for a few moments. This gesture expresses gratitude for the gifts of God's love and presence in your life. Pause like this, allowing yourself a moment to feel thankful for God's good gifts. As you hold your hands in this position, just a few inches in front of your face, whisper, "Thank you, thank you, thank you," for as long as you like.
- We know God's love is meant to be shared, which we do whenever we show love to others, act kindly to them, or help a friend in need. To express this desire to share God's love, lower your arms and swing your arms left and right, like you are flinging seeds onto a field. You can twist your body as you do this, making the gesture big, because you want to spread the seed of God's love far and wide. As you do this, say, "God, I want to share your life with others. Help me do that!" Let yourself really feel the freedom and energy of this gesture as your arms swing right and left.
- Finally, lift your arms above your head with your fingers spread and your palms facing upward. This is a gesture of praise to God. As you do, look upward and say, "God, I praise you with all that I have and all that I am," or, simply, "Praise you, praise you, praise you." Do this for as long as it feels meaningful and comfortable.
- If you'd like, repeat the whole prayer, letting each gesture flow into the next until it becomes one flowing movement of receiving, giving thanks, sharing, and praising. When you are done, let your arms rest at your sides, and once again get a sense of your whole body as you stand before God who is still smiling on you—perhaps a particularly wide smile after watching your body prayer! Finish by whispering, "Amen."

VARIATIONS

- You can experiment and make up your own gestures for this prayer. What gestures are meaningful to you and can help you express your desire to receive God's love, give God thanks, share God's love with others, and offer your life to God in praise?
- You can do body prayer in a group as well. While some might be self-conscious at first, it's important to remember that this is not a contest to see who can do it best, and there is no need to even look at or comment on the way others are doing it.
- Try making up your own prayers. Maybe you want to think about how you would express sorrow to God for something you did that hurt someone or wonder and awe at God's creation. What other prayers might you want to express with your body?

Rooted and Reaching

Scripture invites us to think of those who grow in the spiritual life, who learn to trust God as a friend, as deeply rooted trees. The prophet Jeremiah says of those who trust in the Lord, "They shall be like a tree planted by water, sending out its roots by the stream. It shall not fear when heat comes and its leaves shall stay green; in the year of drought it is not anxious, and it does not cease to bear fruit" (17:7-8). It's a suggestive image of someone with the roots of their faith planted in God—they grow and flourish, whatever challenges life brings. I appreciate how this image reflects the truth that life will bring heat and drought; adversities are unavoidable, but a life rooted in God can flourish, nonetheless.

One of the claims of the Christian faith is that our lives, by our very existence, are rooted in God. Julian of Norwich, the fourteenth-century mystic, said that God is the "ground from which we have all our life."[16] And the twentieth-century theologian Paul Tillich argued that God is the "ground of being."[17] All that we have and all that we are arise out of our relationship with God.

But the image of a tree also points to our aspirations: We want to grow and bear fruit in this life we've been given. As adults we long for this for the kids in our lives—that they might discover a faith that helps them to grow up into their truest selves, to stretch out the limbs of their lives and bear fruit. A tree grows and bears fruit, and it remains steady against storms, all because its roots reach deeply into fertile soil, drawing water, nutrients, and oxygen from the earth. It pulls all of that up and sends it out through the branches and leaves that reach toward the sun.

This bodily way of praying invites kids to physically enact the spiritual truth that prayer helps us stay rooted in God and grow, so that our own lives reach toward God in love. With their bodies, kids get to imagine being rooted in God's love and grace and then act out their own growth and maturation, as they stretch toward the heavens.

THE PRACTICE

- Stand with your feet shoulder-width apart and planted solidly on the ground. Don't rock back and forth, but simply stand, sturdy like a tree. Bring your attention to how your whole body feels as you stand and notice that feeling. What does it feel like to stand there, sturdy and strong?
- Now imagine God looking at you, smiling, thinking, "What a magnificent tree I have made—rooted in my love and stretching toward me in love!" Stand still for a few moments enjoying the thought of God smiling at you.
- Bend down with your hands reaching toward your toes. If you can touch your toes, do that. As you do this, imagine that your arms and legs are roots, stretching deeply into the ground. Imagine

that the ground is God's love and your roots are extending far into that love.

- Now slowly stand up straight, letting your hands gently rise along your legs—across your ankles, shins, knees, and thighs. As you do this, imagine that God's love, grace, and strength are rising within you and nourishing you.
- Keep raising your hands, slowly, past your waist and your chest, past your shoulders, until they have passed your head, and then stretch upwards as far as you can, your palms open to the sky, as if you are reaching toward God, toward heaven. Imagine that you are a tree, and your strong branches, full of leaves, are stretching toward the sun. Pause like this and feel your body as you stretch your arms—your tree limbs—to God.
- Now slowly bring your hands back down, as if you are receiving God's love, letting it flow into your body from above. Reverse the movement, bringing your hands down, past your head and shoulder and neck, until they again rest at your side. As you do this, think about how you are rooted in God's love, and it is rising up within you. Think about how your life is stretching toward God, receiving God's love from above.
- Repeat this prayer practice a few times, continuing to imagine the love of God rising up within you and receiving the love of God from above and bringing it back down into your life.
- When you have finished, let your arms rest at your sides and bring your attention once again to your body. How does it feel now? Does it feel different? More alive and energized? You might want to end by whispering a prayer, something like, "Thank you God for your love that my life grows out of. Help me keep growing and reaching for you."

VARIATIONS

- Do this prayer in the morning as a prayer to start your day. Try it first thing after getting out of bed. The stretching can help wake you up, and it can be a good reminder that as you go through your day you want to be rooted in God and reaching toward God.
- Try this practice with a group, with someone, either another kid or an adult, leading and sharing the instructions. After the prayer practice is complete, stand in a circle and briefly share what it was like. What was it like to imagine yourself—and feel yourself—being rooted in God's love and reaching toward God's love?
- Add words to the movement of this prayer. As you stretch toward the ground, say out loud, "I am rooted in God's love." As you begin to stand and stretch upward, say, "I am reaching toward God's love." As you bring your hands back down, say, "I am receiving God's love into my life." You can vary the words by replacing "God's love" with "God's peace," "God's life," or "God's grace," depending on what feels meaningful at the time.

Body Compassion

When someone asked Jesus what the greatest commandment was, his answer was succinct and unequivocal: Love God with all you've got. He went on to name the second most important commandment: "You shall love your neighbor as yourself" (Mark 12:28-31).

Sometimes, however, we don't love ourselves well, and kids can struggle with loving and accepting themselves, especially their bodies. As kids approach middle school they receive more and more exposure to idealized body images. These images convey not-so-subtle suggestions about how their own bodies should look, making kids increasingly self-conscious about their bodies.

This prayer practice invites kids to experience their bodies in a compassionate, nonjudgmental way. It allows them to welcome, with love, their own bodies into the world just as God, who delights in them, made and welcomes their bodies into the world. This prayer practice helps kids to learn, deep down, that *there is no body that God is ashamed of.*

When the Son of God came to earth, he took on a human body—he *welcomed* a human body—and in so doing showed God's love for all that makes us human, including our bodies. That's why we call the mystery at the heart of the Christian faith the Incarnation—the very enfleshment of God. In his ministry, Jesus offered compassion and care to the bodies of so many others. It wouldn't be a stretch to say that paying loving attention to the bodies of others and offering them compassion was close to the heart of his ministry.

Kids can grow in their own care for others when they accept their whole selves—body, mind, and soul—with compassion and love, just as God does.

THE PRACTICE

- Find a comfortable place to sit where you can stay alert, but where your body will also feel supported and at ease. As you are getting comfortable, imagine God smiling at you, welcoming you into this time of prayer. God is so happy to spend this time with you!
- Begin to breathe slowly and naturally. Focus your attention on your breathing, feeling the air flow into your lungs and your belly expand, and then feeling the air flow back out. When random thoughts pop into your mind, just bring your attention back to your breathing. Do this for a minute or two.
- Now allow your attention to widen to take in your whole body, like you are moving from a zoomed-in focus on your breathing to a zoomed-out view where you can sense your whole body, right

where it is. Feel the weight of your bottom in the chair; feel the fabric of your clothes against your skin; feel your back pressed against the back of the chair. Notice the position of your hands and feet. Become aware of all of this. You don't need to change anything; just notice. If your mind wanders as you are doing this, simply bring it back to sensing your body as a whole. Do this for a minute or two.

- As you sit, giving your attention to your body, let yourself begin to feel love for your body and for all the amazing things it can do—eat, sleep, play, exercise, and so much more! Rest in this feeling of love and gratitude as you sit, sensing your body. If you want, you can think or whisper the words, "Thank you, God, for this body of mine."
- As you do this, it's possible that you will notice aspects of your body that you have a hard time loving and being grateful for. Maybe your body can't do all the things other kids can do. Maybe you struggle in gym class or have to sit out of games sometimes. Maybe you have an injury that is keeping you from being active. Perhaps someone has made fun of you, or you have felt that you are not pretty enough or handsome enough. These are hard feelings. It's not wrong to have them. If you are having any of these thoughts or feelings, try to be very tender with yourself, as you would with a good friend who is feeling bad about themselves. Remember that God loves you and thinks you are amazing just as you are. If these feelings are strong, you may want to share them with a grown-up you trust after this prayer practice ends.
- Return your attention to your body and then let it move to different parts of your body, like a flashlight moving over your body. Imagine that you are sending beams of compassion, tenderness, and love to that part of your body. Send love and compassion to your feet . . . your knees and legs . . . your hips . . . your belly

and chest . . . your arms, shoulder, and neck . . . your head . . . your back. Take your time doing this, zooming in on each part of your body, sending imaginary rays of love and compassion, remembering the whole time that God holds you with great love and compassion.

- As you finish this practice of prayer, say a prayer to God thanking God for this body of yours and asking God to help you keep loving and caring for your body as much as God does.

VARIATIONS

- You can shorten this practice by focusing on just one part of the body, on one occasion focusing on your feet, another time giving attention to your hands, and so forth.
- You can do this practice with a group, sitting in a circle with eyes closed, and having a grown-up lead the practice. When the prayer practice is complete, the grown-up can lead a conversation about how this practice went and why it can be so hard to love and have compassion for our bodies.
- Try this practice while lying in bed before going to sleep, letting the feelings of compassion and love for your body lead you gently into sleep. (Getting sleep is a great way to love our bodies too!)

Body Compassion

Mary Clare says . . .

It was nine o'clock on a Sunday night when I lay down in my bed for my mom to lead me in this prayer practice. My body was admittedly hurting from a busy day, a marching band competition that went late the night before, and a tennis injury I'd been recovering from. With all that had been going on in my life, it was hard to take a moment and appreciate my body letting me do all the things I love.

A few years ago, when I was younger, I enjoyed doing mindfulness meditations with my dad out of a meditation book for kids. These mediations would have me focus on my breathing or do a body scan to just be aware of my body and help me relax. This body compassion prayer practice is similar to those meditations, except with this practice I can also think about how God loves me just the way I am, holds me, and smiles at how perfectly made I am.

Three times during this practice I started laughing. I think it was out of love and joy for this body that God gave me, this body that lets me play tennis, play my instruments, sing, dance, read, study for tests, and sleep. This body may hurt and be tired, but only because it works so hard day and night to let me do the things I enjoy the most. This body lets me hug my loved ones and laugh—hard, often, and sometimes even during prayer!

I was so glad to finally take the time to not only appreciate and love my body but also thank God for making me perfectly in God's image.

The Lord's Prayer

In the Sermon on the Mount, Jesus gives instructions about praying. He first tells his listeners not to show off by praying in public but to find a private place to pray (Matt. 6:6). Then he tells them to keep their prayers short and simple, not heaping up phrase upon phrase, as if more words will get God to hear them (Matt. 6:7-8). As an alternative to lengthy, wordy prayers, he tells them to pray a simple prayer, with just a handful of phrases, a prayer that has become known as the Lord's Prayer. Since then, this has become the prayer most often prayed by Christians both corporately and in private. One important first-century document instructs Christians to pray the Lord's Prayer three times a day.[18] The Lord's Prayer can be found in the Gospels of Matthew, Mark, and Luke, with slight variations among them.

One of the challenges of repeating prayers that have been memorized is that we can recite them on autopilot, no longer appreciating the meaning of what we are saying. We can pray the Lord's Prayer without considering how powerful it is that we are asking for God's own kingdom—the world the way God wants it—to invade our own world. We don't consider the utter reliance on God, moment by moment, expressed when we ask God for daily bread. We don't experience the power of receiving forgiveness from God and offering forgiveness to others, and the link between the two, and we don't allow our hearts to rise in authentic praise when we ascribe glory to God at the end of the prayer. Instead, we utter the prayer mindlessly.

Praying the Lord's Prayer with our bodies can help bring renewed attention to the prayer, and it can be especially meaningful to kids. By giving them ways to engage their bodies while offering this prayer, enacting gestures that symbolize the meaning of the words, we present an avenue for them to reconnect with the prayer, to make it their own, and to pray it with their whole selves, not just their lips.

There are different versions of the Lord's Prayer. In what follows, I use the version most common in Protestant congregations, and I indicate the one place where these traditions most commonly differ. A newer version of the prayer, called the Ecumenical Version, readily available online, can easily be substituted. This newer version might make more sense to kids, but it's less likely they will already have it memorized.

THE PRACTICE

- Find a comfortable place to sit, with plenty of room to move your arms up and down, and left and right. After getting comfortable, sit in the silence for a few moments, being thankful for this opportunity to communicate with God. Imagine that God is smiling at you, so glad for this time to spend with you. Sit in the silence for as long as you feel comfortable.

- As you begin to say the Lord's Prayer, make the following gestures along with each phrase of the prayer:

  "Our Father, who art in heaven . . ."

  As you say this phrase, bring your palms together in front of your heart with your fingers pointing upward.

  ". . . hallowed be thy name."

  Raise your arms forward and upward in a "V" shape with your palms facing upward in a gesture of praise and openness to God, honoring God's holiness.

  "Thy kingdom come, thy will be done . . ."

  Lower your hands slowly to your lap, resting your hands on your thighs with your palms still facing upward, as if you want to receive God's kingdom as it comes.

  ". . . on earth as it is in heaven."

  Bend forward and reach your arms toward the ground, touching it if you can, indicating your desire for God's heavenly kingdom—the way God wants the world to be to be fully present on earth, and that you want to be a part of it!

  "Give us this day our daily bread . . ."

  Hold your hands out in front of you in a cupped position, one hand on top of the other, as if someone were about to place a piece of bread in your hands. This is a gesture that symbolizes your reliance upon God and your readiness to receive God's blessings and gifts in your life.

". . . and forgive us our trespasses as we forgive those who trespass against us" or "forgive us our debts as we forgive our debtors."

With your arms remaining forward and your hands remaining in a cupped, ready-to-receive position, bow your head. This gesture symbolizes your desire to receive God's forgiveness, but also to offer forgiveness to others with outstretched arms.

"And lead us not into temptation . . ."

Stretch your arms out straight in front of you, with your palms facing forward, as if to say "stop" to someone approaching you.

". . . but deliver us from evil . . ."

As you pray this phrase, spread your arms wide open to your sides, as if they have just broken out of chains, and it feels so good to be free!

"For thine is the kingdom, and the power, and the glory forever."

Once again, raise your arms forward and upward in a "V" shape, with your palms facing upward, in a gesture of praise and openness to God, honoring God's holiness and giving glory to God.

"Amen."

As you say this final word, bring your palms together in front of your heart with your fingers pointing upward, the gesture with which the prayer began.

- Now spend a few moments appreciating this opportunity to be with God and pray with your body before getting out of your chair.

VARIATIONS

- Do this in a group while sitting in a circle. This can be an excellent way to begin or end a Sunday school class or a youth group meeting. After the prayer, with the guidance of an adult, have a conversation about the meaning of each of the phrases of the Lord's Prayer.
- Do this daily, perhaps sitting on the edge of a bed first thing in the morning or before going to bed at night.
- Once you feel like you have a deeper understanding of the different phrases within the prayer, experiment by creating your own gestures for the prayer. Show them to someone and tell them why these gestures are meaningful to you.

chapter sixteen

Ways to Pray in Nature

Nature Walk

When I talk to adults about when they feel most open or connected to God in prayer, many of them say, "When I'm in nature." I remember a woman who told me that her primary method of prayer was sitting on her back patio each morning with a cup of coffee, enjoying the sights and sounds of God's creation—listening to the birds, squirrels, and bees; the wind, the rain, and the trees. That's where and how she found relationship with God.

Marjorie Thompson, in her book *Soul Feast*, says that nature is one of the primary ways we can listen to God.[19] God's creation can be a vehicle for us to recognize and nourish our relationship with God. Psalm 19 declares, "The heavens are telling the glory of God; and the firmament proclaims his handiwork" (Psalm 19:1). God is present in God's creation, loving and upholding all things in existence. Creation knows this and praises God for it.

Unfortunately, many kids these days suffer from what I've heard referred to as "nature deficit disorder"—the consequence of kids spending less time outside and more time indoors and on screens. This broken connection with creation not only affects kids psychologically, but it also leaves them cut off from an essential way of experiencing awe in God's presence, feeling God's love, and knowing they belong within the wider web of creation. Praying with nature helps kids find wholeness by taking their place in the greater household of God's marvelous world.

And it can all begin with a nature walk. Whether this occurs at a local nature preserve or along a suburban sidewalk, any place with a few trees, a glimpse of the sky, the blur of a running squirrel, or even a weed pushing through a crack can become opportunity to encounter God. A prayerful walk in nature is a simple way to introduce prayer in the outdoors.

This kind of walk is not primarily about talking to God (though that's not off limits; remember, there is no right way to do this). It's not even about trying to hear something *from* God. It's about fostering communion and connection with God through openness to what God has made—this stunningly beautiful, resilient world.

Since this kind of prayer primarily involves attention and awareness, cell phones should stay put away during this practice. A prayer walk is best done in silence; for folks who do it together, sharing and conversation can happen at the end.

PRAYER GUIDE

- Begin by standing outdoors where the walk will start. As you stand there, with eyes either open or closed, imagine God smiling at you, and spend a few moments enjoying that thought. If you are in a place where you can feel the sun or a breeze on your face, imagine that sensation as a sign of God's smiling love, reaching out to touch you. Say a short prayer letting God know that as you walk you simply want to be open to God during this time spent in creation.

- Before you start walking, get in touch with your senses. Wake up to what is around you: What do you see? What do you hear? What do you feel—the sun, a breeze, a drizzle of rain? What do you smell?
- Now walk. It's that simple. Walk slowly, this is not a race. Better to walk a short distance slowly, taking in God's world through all your senses, than to hurry along, covering a great distance but missing everything. Pay attention. Look around. Are there ants on the sidewalk? Pause and notice their busyness. Are there chipmunks scurrying in the grass? Notice how alert they are. Listen. Do you hear a distant lawnmower or a woodpecker tapping on a tree? As you walk slowly, take it all in.
- At some point you'll get lost in thought. You'll start thinking about something, and though you will still be in nature, it will seem like your mind is someplace else. When you notice this, just come back to the world around you and start paying attention again. Ask yourself what you see, hear, smell, feel.
- When the walk is over, take a moment to reflect: What did you notice that stuck out to you? Did you see anything that reminded you of God's love and faithfulness? Did you encounter anything that was beautiful? Did you ever feel a sense of awe and wonder?
- As you wrap up your reflection, whisper another prayer to God, thanking God for this world you've been placed in. Thank God for all that you saw, heard, and felt. Let God know if you intend to spend more time connecting with God's love through creation.

VARIATIONS

- Do this with a group of people. Stay silent as you walk (seriously, don't talk to each other!) and then share with each other what you noticed or what it meant to you afterward.

- Not everyone can walk easily. You can do this kind of prayer sitting as well as walking. Pull a chair into the front yard and have a nature *sit*.
- Do this prayer practice along the same path several times in one week—at different times of the day if you can—and keep a record in a journal or notebook about what you notice. How did what you noticed change over the week? What different things did you notice each day?

Look What I Found!

This prayer practice is related to nature walks, but it doesn't involve following a path and can be done almost anywhere outside, wherever a bit of nature is pushing through. This practice is aimed at helping kids approach God's creation with imagination, as they look for an object that captures their attention and speaks to them about God, God's love for the world, and God's love for them. Jesus modeled this way of interacting with God's creation when he pointed out how lilies, ravens, and mustard seeds all suggest the ways of God and God's kingdom.

Jesus encouraged his followers to notice objects in nature, meditate on them, and let them inform us of God's care, not only for the non-human parts creation, but for humanity as well. He called attention to birds and let them be reminders of God's compassion as he entered Jerusalem; he gestured to rocks, affirming that they praise God even when we don't. In this way, he gave his listeners permission to read the book of creation and ask, "What does it say to us about God?" Kids will pay attention, notice, listen, and imagine as they look for something in nature that declares God's goodness and love. They will find a way of communicating with God *through* nature.

When kids are invited to find and then reflect on an object in creation—a feather, a rock, a rose petal—they can allow their imaginations to be lifted to God so that they can come to know God better through what God has made.

If you are doing this prayer practice with kids, here's an important reminder: Trust their imaginations and resist the urge to influence their thinking or to correct them. This type of intrusion might make them think that they have somehow done prayer wrong. If a kid is sharing with you about what they found and how it reminds them of God, stay curious and listen—God might be speaking to you through them.

PRAYER PRACTICE

- Go outside and simply stand there. You might want to hold your arms out to your sides as if you are welcoming into your life all that God has made. As you stand there (with your arms out—who cares if your neighbors see you!), imagine God smiling at you, looking at you in love. God is *so* in love with you; the very thought of you makes God smile. Ask God to help you look at God's creation with an open heart and help you come to know God better through what God has made.
- Now walk around outside with your eyes open for any object that captures your attention. There's no hurry here. Take your time. Don't force it. Roam around and stay open until something draws your curiosity. What do you see?
- When you see something that captures your attention, pick it up if you can, or, if the object is too large to hold, stand still and look at it. Is it a rock, a clover, a dandelion? Is it a feather, a stick, or a tree? A bee? A leaf? It can be almost anything!
- Cradle what you have found in your hands and carry it someplace where you can sit down (unless it's too big, then stay where you are). Maybe there's a tree you can rest your back against, or you might want to sit down right in the middle of the yard.

- Gaze at the object carefully and with an open mind. If this is the object you were drawn to, trust that the Holy Spirit can teach you about God's love through it. Where does your imagination go when you look at the object and feel it in your hands? How does this object remind you of God's love, grace, and faithfulness? What characteristics of the object make you think about God? For instance, the hardness of a rock might make you think about how God's love is as solid as a rock; a delicate flower might make you think about how God cares for delicate things (do you feel delicate sometimes?); a weed might make you think about how God cares for things (and people) that others don't want or like. There are no right answers. You are using your imagination to read the book of God's creation.
- If nothing comes to you, that's fine too. Just admire what you've found and talk to God about it, thanking God for the thing you hold in your hands and for the marvelous diversity of creation.
- Continue with this prayer practice for as long as you like. When you are finished, whisper a prayer to God, thanking God for showing you a glimpse of who God is through God's creation. Tell God that you want to keep growing closer to God, and that you are happy for creation to help you do that. Finally, place the object back where you found it.

VARIATIONS

- Try this with others. Set a timer for ten minutes then look around. When the time is up, gather in a circle—kids and adults together and share your objects and how they helped you imagine God's love.

- Draw a picture of the object you found and next to it write one word that can remind you of what you thought about as you reflected on the object.
- Do this several times in one week and keep the objects in a box. At the end of the week, go through the contents of the box. As you look at each item, remember how it helped you draw closer to God.

Mary Clare says . . .

This year, as August faded into September, I grew very busy—you know how those first few weeks of school can be. At the same time, our region experienced a long time without any rain. In my hurry from one place to another I didn't notice that the grass turned yellow or that the leaves fell way too early. I did notice the 80-degree weather that lingered too far into September, but only because I had to check the forecast daily to know whether to wear shorts or pants.

One evening my parents and I ventured into the neighborhood nature reserve at the end of a tiring day. I had many thoughts and plans swirling around in my head, so I was a little distracted. But as my dad explained this prayer practice, I tried to focus my energy on nature and God. He also said that we could take pictures of anything that caught our attention on our walk so that we could share them with each other later.

Over the first couple minutes of our walk, I realized just how dry and still everything was, save for a chipmunk scurrying up a tree. The creek was dangerously low, there were no birds or insects in sight, and all the plants that should have been green were brown. It was kind of sad, to be honest.

But then I came across the stump of a recently fallen cherry tree with a blazing orange-red center. It almost glowed against the colorless background of the trail, and it was beautiful. It matched the color of the sunset that peeked through the trees and made me remember that God brings us beauty, even through a fallen tree concealed within a barren nature reserve. The inside of the stump was fresh and alive with color as if it had never experienced a drought. What a miracle!

At the end of our walk, my parents and I sat at a picnic table and shared photos of the things we'd found. My dad showed off a bright green leaf laying in the middle of the path. My mom offered a picture of the intricate twisted tree trunks that lined the path. She added, "God made them beautiful and unlike any other tree trunk." These were things I had not noticed but did on our walk back. I appreciated the different views on how God works in nature so that I could see it too.

Once we were out of the reserve, my dad said, "You know, studies show that spending just ten minutes in nature boosts your mood and makes you happier." I think that's right. I hadn't been outside and able to appreciate God's creation in so long, and that little walk made me happier. But I also think taking the time to find the good that God brings has the same effect, even—maybe especially—if you have to search for it.

Starry, Starry Night

Few things can inspire a sense of awe like looking into the night sky, contemplating the magnitude of the universe, and admiring the beauty of those distant, twinkling lights. It can remind us how small we are in comparison to this vastness and lead us to marvel at God's infinite love for us. Has there been a more universal spiritual practice than looking into the heavens in contemplative wonder? Kids do it quite naturally!

Christians believe that the God who spoke the universe into being is the same God who stepped out of eternity and into time out of love—all to be with us, to share life with us. This is God's deepest desire. We can connect with the God who loves us when we allow the immensity of the universe—the black holes and distant galaxies, the comets and moons and meteors—to remind us how comparatively small we are. And yet God regards us with an infinite love that exceeds, beyond measure, the space between and beyond the galaxies.

In other words, our natural desire to gaze at the sky can become prayer when we gaze with the intention of being with God and learning about God's love for us through it. This also gives us a chance to praise God for all God has made and marvel at God's own majesty, creativity, and power. It gives us a moment to think about all that there is—and to know that God holds it lovingly, moment by moment.

This prayer practice opens space for kids to shift their natural awe of the night sky into intentional prayer, helping them move from admiring the stars to admiring God through the stars. It's a staple of Christian theology that knowledge of God and knowledge of ourselves go hand-in-hand. By prayerfully enjoying a starry night, we can grow in both. In humility, we can acknowledge our relative insignificance in the face of the majesty of the universe, and we can allow that truth to lead us to the mystery that the universe's Creator knows and loves each one of us just as we are.

Kids aren't too young to contemplate these mysteries. Along the way, we might find they become *our* teachers and guides.

PRAYER GUIDE

- Find a comfortable blanket that can get a little dirty. Take a pillow if you need it or two blankets for some cushion on the ground—being comfortable is important. You can do this where you live, especially if it's a clear night and there aren't a lot of outdoor lights. The darker, the better.

- Lay down on your blankets and let your eyes take in the sky. Don't force anything; just take it all in. As you do this, imagine that God is smiling at you. God is delighted that you are taking this time to be with God, and even more, that you are taking time to enjoy the universe God made. Take a moment to appreciate God's delight in you. You might want to whisper a prayer, something like, "God, it's good to be here, with you. Thank you for the beauty of the night sky."
- Now look at the sky. Go where your eyes take you. Can you identify any constellations—the Big or Little Dippers, perhaps, or Orion's Belt? What patterns do *you* see in the stars? If you were to connect some of the stars, what picture would it make? Spend some time in this open, creative inspection of the sky.
- Then notice what you are *feeling* as you wonder at the stars. There is no right way to feel. Do you feel small? Do you feel a sense of awe? Are you moved by the beauty of it? Are you puzzled by where it all came from, what the stars are made of, or how far outer space extends? Does observing the night sky give you a sense of peace with your place in the universe, or does it stir up anxiety in you? Any of these thoughts, feelings, and questions are okay.
- After you have paid attention to how all of this makes you feel, then turn your mind to thoughts of God. Can you believe that God made all this and loves it? Can you believe that God is bigger than the whole universe?
- Think about how God, who created each star and all the galaxies (and loves them), loves you too and created you and knows how many hairs are on your head. Can you imagine that God is looking at you right now in wonder just as you are looking at the stars?

- Finally, notice that the stars give light in the darkness of the sky. Remember that you too are part of God's light. How did your life shine a little light in the world today? Perhaps through an act of kindness or a word of comfort for a friend? How do you think God is inviting you to shine tomorrow? Do you have a friend, a teacher, or someone in your family who needs a little of your light?
- Lie here for as long as you feel like it and for as long as you are enjoying this practice. Lose yourself in the wonder and beauty of it all. When you are ready to go back inside, talk to God silently (or out loud) about what this time of prayer has meant to you.

VARIATIONS

- When you finish, go inside and write down one word that captures what you are taking away from this practice or write down how you sensed God leading you to shine your light tomorrow.
- During the next day, continue to bring your mind back to this experience of prayer. If you have any down time, use your imagination to return to what you were feeling, thinking, or sensing about God as you prayed with the stars.
- You can do this with family or friends or with members of your church community. Meet at someone's house, enjoy some fellowship, then have someone lead those who are present in this prayer practice.

Icky Weather

Weather affects all of us. Our family moved to Pittsburgh a number of years ago after living for fifteen years in the sunny South, and I still haven't adjusted to the long, gray winters. Gray is the worst. I also haven't adjusted to the hills, lovely in the fall, but which make winter driving an anxious nightmare. The gray affects my mood, and the snow can box me in. Then there is July, which I have come to think of as Pittsburgh's monsoon season. Given the hills and the many creeks, every time there's a hefty rain, flash flood warnings are triggered, and I still don't know where it's safe to drive.

Often weather keeps us from doing what we want to do. This is a place where adults can easily empathize with the frustration of kids. No one likes it when icky weather cancels plans. As I write this, it's Halloween. It's going to be cold this evening, but not so cold that kids can't haunt the neighborhoods seeking candy. But it's not uncommon for snow or rain to squash trick-or-treating plans. Last weekend was chilly and damp, and Mary Clare told me she wasn't able to get outside and move her body—there was just no opportunity to take a long walk or run the track at the nearby high school. She said she could feel the difference. Icky weather got in the way.

Still, I have learned that we can bring our frustrations into prayer, even frustration about plans upended by bad weather. We can hold our annoyances in prayer before God and look for God's grace in these situations. We can be honest with ourselves and with God about how we are feeling. Sometimes we might discover that when we bring our frustration over icky weather—or any other situation—into our relationship with God, our relationship to those feelings of frustration can change. We can open ourselves to God's presence in that moment and also open ourselves to the possibilities that God is making available for us, even when bad weather rules out some options.

This way of praying with nature allows kids to create space to share their frustrations with God. It's not limited to feelings about the weather though—it also works for other areas of their lives: feeling upset about not making the team; disappointment over a bad grade; anger that a case of the flu caused a birthday party to be canceled. Over time kids (and adults!) may learn to face all kinds of frustrating situations with an increasing sense of emotional balance. What a gift to learn that we can bring our sadness, impatience, and even anger into that safe place of prayer with God, let God cradle us in those feelings, and allow ourselves to be open to the possibility that God's grace is always being revealed to us.

This prayer practice can be used on any occasion when the weather outside is getting in the way. Of course, if it's a snow day, the kids might not be frustrated at all, but that might be when the grown-ups in the house need to turn to this prayer practice.

PRAYER PRACTICE

- Find a place where you can see the weather outside, perhaps standing or sitting in front of a window. If you have a covered patio (and it's not too cold), do this on the patio. The closer you can get to the weather, the better. Now observe the weather from wherever you are and imagine that God is smiling on you. You might be feeling frustration or anger because the weather is keeping you from doing something fun. Remember God can see all the emotions roiling inside of you and still looks at you with love. The weather changes, but the smile you bring to God's face never will. Do your best to try to connect with that truth in your heart.
- Then observe the weather. Watch and listen, as deeply as you can. What do you see and hear? If you are outside or if a window or door is open, what do you feel? Can you feel a breeze? The cold air or the hot, humid air? Can you feel mist on your face? Can you hear thunder booming or wind gusts shaking the leaves?
- As you watch, notice how you are feeling. Are feelings of annoyance, frustration, or anger showing up inside of you? Simply observe these feelings just like you observed the weather. Look at them and feel them without thinking about them too much or judging them. Feeling this way is not right or wrong; it's just how

you feel right now. Be aware of that. Just as the weather outside changes—the rain lightens up; the wind dies down—so does the weather of your feelings. As you observe, you may notice the frustration grow stronger or get weaker. You may want to say what you are noticing out loud to God, something like, "God, I see that I am upset. I feel this mostly in my stomach," or "God, I'm noticing that the angry feelings are calming down a bit."

- Now bring your attention back to the weather outside. How is it changing? What are you noticing? As you watch, allow yourself to start thinking about how the weather is part of God's creation. Remind yourself that all things pass and change, all things come and go. This weather will too. Then, either silently or aloud, ask God to help you to see what possibilities the weather is creating for you: Is there something you *can* do now—inside, at home, or wherever you happen to be—that could bring joy to you or to someone you love? Is there something that you have been putting off (for instance, cleaning your room or doing homework) that this weather might be giving you the opportunity to tackle? What if you did nothing but just stood and watched the weather for a while, letting it absorb your thoughts and attention?
- When you feel ready to quit, say a short prayer, something like, "God of sun and blue skies, God of rain and snow, God of summer and winter, here I am watching bad weather. But here you are too. Thank you for your love and presence and bless all those like me who are feeling frustrated by this weather. Open us to new possibilities."

VARIATIONS

- When you are done, find someone and talk with them about the weather. Ask them how they are feeling about it (their feelings might be very different from yours) or get in touch with a friend and ask them how they are doing.
- If the weather is bad but not dangerous do this prayer practice outside in the middle of it all, so that you can really feel the weather. (You might need an adult's permission).
- When the weather changes, repeat the exercise even if you are no longer feeling frustrated. What are you feeling now? How does the change in the weather affect what you talk to God about?

chapter seventeen
Ways to Pray Together

Little Church

During the COVID shutdowns, our family, like so many others, felt robbed of worship with our community since we could no longer attend church in person on Sunday mornings. As a response, we decided to have family worship on Sunday evenings, just the five of us (two parents, two high schoolers, and Mary Clare, then in fifth grade). We'd sit in the family room, light a candle, sing a simple song, and read and discuss a passage of scripture. We'd end by praying for one another and passing the peace of Christ. The practice was remarkably simple; it required no elaborate preparations and no props besides a candle, a match, a Bible, and our own willing spirits. We found that these moments spent connecting with God and each other helped sustain us through the challenging pandemic days. Sometimes we wondered why we hadn't started sooner, why it took a global crisis to nudge our family into this kind of prayerful circle.

In the seventeenth century, a German Lutheran pastor named Philip Jacob Spener sought to continue the reforms of the Protestant Reformation. He argued that the Reformation did a wonderful job of adjusting theology and church doctrine to align with scripture, but Christian life and practice still needed continued attention. The church was not as vibrant as Spener thought it should be, and he believed that people lacked a sense of vital connection with God. Among his many suggestions for reform—laid out in a small book called *Pia Desideria*—was the suggestion that Christians should gather in small groups to pray, learn, and grow together—to support and encourage one another in the life of faith. Spener believed that a household could become a school of faith formation as families pray and read scripture together.[20] These household gatherings later became known as *ecclesiolae in ecclesia*, a Latin phrase that means "little churches within the church."

I find Spener's notion encouraging. The people I live with and share my time with—my family—can be a little church, embodying the truth of Jesus's promise that where "two or three are gathered in my name, I am there among them" (Matt. 18:20). This little church can be comprised of biological relations, chosen family, or close friends. The practice is simple enough that kids can be encouraged to participate and take the lead alongside adults.

Read through the practice below and decide ahead of time who will do what. Who will serve as the leader? Who will light the candle? Who will read scripture, and what passage will be read? Then begin to work through the practice together.

THE PRACTICE

- As the group gathers, sit in a circle facing one another with a candle on a center table. Maybe you are gathering in a family room with a coffee table in the middle or around the dining room table. Have someone light the candle (with adult supervision!) while the group together says, "We light this candle because Jesus is the light of the world."

- The leader can say, "Let's take a few moments of silence to become aware of God's presence. In the silence, imagine that God is smiling on us, gazing on us in tender love." Then allow for twenty or thirty seconds of silence.
- Now have someone read a short passage of scripture. Introduce the reading with the words, "Listen with the ears of your heart to what God is saying." When the reading is finished, the one who read should say, "This is the word of the Lord," and everyone responds, "Thanks be to God!"
- Following the reading, have the group take a few minutes to share where they have experienced God's goodness in their lives lately and what they need God's help with in the coming days. First, the leader should say something like, "Let us share briefly what we want to give God thanks for over the last few days." Each person should have the opportunity to share, but no one should be forced to share.
- Then the leader should ask, "What do we need God's help with in the coming days?" Each person should have the opportunity to share about something in their life that they'd like God's grace to help them with or support them through. Maybe a kid has a test coming up or an audition for a school play; maybe a grown-up has a job interview or a stressful meeting at work in the next few days.
- When it seems like everyone who wants to share has done so, the leader should say, "Let us pray the Lord's Prayer together," and lead those gathered in reciting the Lord's Prayer.
- After praying the Lord's Prayer, the leader can close this time of gathering as a little church by saying, "God's love is with us," with everyone responding, "Thanks be to God!" The leader then invites everyone to stand and share the peace of Christ with each other through hugs, handshakes, and pats on the back, while saying, "The peace of Christ be with you."

VARIATIONS

- This practice has room for flexibility and improvisation. For instance, after lighting the candle the group can sing a song together. This is not a rigid format so feel free to make additions and changes to fit the needs of the group.
- After the scripture reading, invite the group to have a conversation about the passage. The leader can ask something like, "How does this passage of scripture connect with your life right now?" Anyone can share but remember that it is not time to correct kids when they are sharing their thoughts about scripture. Instead, this is the time for adults to be open and accepting of what kids say to foster a sense of trust.
- This practice can be done weekly, on Sunday evenings for instance. It can also be done nightly as a form of evening prayer.

Joys and Concerns

Paul's letter to the Philippians is often called the epistle of joy, because Paul uses words related to joy and rejoicing sixteen times over the course of the letter. Most famously he uses these words near the end where he writes, "Rejoice in the Lord always; again I will say, Rejoice" (4:4).

It's hard to know what it means to rejoice always—I can't imagine a middle schooler rejoicing during a pre-algebra exam for instance (though perhaps there is rejoicing when it is over). But taking time with others to name the ways God is bringing joy into our lives is one way we can practice rejoicing and a way we can come closer to doing it always.

The other name for this practice, of course, is giving thanks. Sometimes we have great joys to share, like when a family member gets released from the hospital after a serious illness. Sometimes our joys are smaller, like when a squirrel recently watched me from a couple feet away as I ate my breakfast outside. Sharing our joy with others can encourage them, strengthen our own faith and make us better at noticing small joys in the moment.

In the same letter, Paul also writes, "Do not worry about anything, but in everything by prayer and supplication with thanksgiving let your requests be made known to God" (4:6). I haven't quite figured out how to not be anxious and be free of all worry, but Paul is suggesting that, along with giving thanks, we should offer our worries to God.

When we invite kids to do this, they might find that their worries get lighter when they share them with God and with others. Some concerns are personal, like an upcoming math test or a rough patch in a friendship, and some are broader, like wars on the other side of the world and natural disasters on the other side of the country. Lifting up these concerns to God in the presence of others can ease the burden of carrying them alone and help grow our trust in a God who knows and cares about what troubles our hearts.

This prayer practice creates the opportunity for kids to join with others—friends and family members of all ages—in naming the good gifts of God that we see in our lives and sharing our burdens with a God we can trust. As scripture says, "Cast all your anxiety on him, because he cares for you" (1 Peter 5:7).

THE PRACTICE

- Gather with a group—it doesn't matter how many—and sit where you can see one another. Someone will need to be the leader. After a leader is selected, the leader should say something like, "Let's take a few moments in silence to imagine God smiling on us and sense the warmth and presence of God's love."
- After the silence, the prayer practice begins with those gathered sharing with one another what has recently brought them joy. There are no right or wrong answers to this question—things

both large and small are appropriate! The leader should get the sharing started by asking, "What do you want to give God thanks for? How has God brought you joy recently?"

- After someone shares, the leader says, "Loving God," to which everyone responds, "We give you thanks." This continues until it seems like everyone who wants to share has been able to.
- Then the leader asks, "What concerns or worries on our hearts do we want to lift before God? How do we need to pray for each other, our community, and our world?" At this point, members of the group are invited to share their worries or concerns. Again, there is no right answer. The things shared can be large or small. They can be personal concerns, concerns for other people you know, or concerns about big issues in the world. There are so many needs and so many things we can pray for. The most important thing is to share concerns that you and others feel burdened by or have been thinking about lately.
- After someone shares, the leader says, "Merciful God," to which everyone responds, "Hear our prayer." This continues until it seems like everyone who wants to share has been able to.
- At this point, the leader says something like, "Let's take a few moments in silence to hold all of these joys and concerns before God and give thanks in our hearts that God hears all of our prayers."
- After a minute or so of silent prayer, the leader concludes, "Let us close by praying together the Lord's Prayer," and then the group prays the Lord's Prayer together.

VARIATIONS

- Find a friend you trust and ask them to be your prayer partner. Commit to getting together once a week (preferably in person, but FaceTime or a phone call works as well) and practice praying this way together. Over time, you will grow to trust one another and value the opportunity to share the joys and concerns that you carry with someone else and with God.

- Your family can try practicing this at the beginning of the evening meal, with each person having the opportunity to share one joy and one concern.
- Make this a personal practice by keeping a journal. Every night before bed, write one joy from the day—this might be the high point of the day or something smaller—and then sit with the memory of that moment, giving thanks to God. Then write one concern—perhaps the low point of the day—and then sit for a few moments in silence offering this concern to God.

Before Bed

A few years ago, Marcy Clare bought a small metal box packed with prayer cards. Each card was printed with a psalm, a few verses of scripture, or a prayer—some of them well-known. Many nights, as I was putting her to bed, we'd shuffle through the cards and pick out the prayers that we liked. One of them was a favorite of mine, a prayer attributed to the fourth-century theologian and North African bishop, Augustine of Hippo (though he may not have written it himself). I knew the prayer from a prayer book I had used regularly many years earlier. In that book the prayer goes like this:

> Keep watch, dear LORD, with all who work or watch or weep this night, and give Your angels charge over those who sleep. Tend the sick, we pray, and give rest to the weary; soothe the suffering and bless the dying; pity the afflicted and shield the joyous; and all for Your love's sake. Amen.[21]

Sometimes we would pray this prayer together; sometimes we would talk about what the different phrases mean. I remember once sharing with Mary Clare how much I liked the phrase "shield the joyous"—it seems so thoughtful to ask God to sustain someone's joy.

Weeks after Mary Clare's purchase, my mother was nearing the end of her life. One night, as we were praying this prayer, I paused after the phrase "bless the dying," and I mentioned my mother. I hoped God would make God's presence known to her so that she might have courage to face this final leg of her life's journey.

After that, we would occasionally pause after other phrases in this prayer and take time to mention people we knew who were experiencing what those phrases described. In that way, the prayer guided and supported us as we remembered to pray for the people in our lives. This practice gave Mary Clare the opportunity to pray for her friends, teachers, and her own family. There were times we even mentioned ourselves as we prayed.

This practice is simple, and, after a while, kids will have this beautiful prayer memorized. It will become an aid to their praying for the rest of their lives, tucked safely in their memory.

THE PRACTICE

- If you have a grown-up who puts you to bed, use this practice with them as you are going to bed. If they no longer do this, you can do this practice before bed with anyone in your household who will join you.
- Along with the person who is joining you in this prayer, take some time to sit and welcome God's presence. Imagine that God is looking at you with delight at the end of this day, so glad to have accompanied you through everything you've done and now eager

to bless you before sleep. For a few moments, simply sit with this thought and rest in it.

- Then begin to pray this prayer out loud, one phrase at a time, praying for people you know—friends, family members, acquaintances—who might be experiencing the things to which the various phrases of the prayer refer. Use the following guide as a help in this:

  "Keep watch, dear Lord, with all who work or watch or weep this night . . ."

  Do you know anyone who is working this evening or keeping watch (that is, waiting expectantly for something)? Do you know anyone who is deeply sad? Say their names now, asking God to "keep watch" with them, which means to join them in what they are going through.

  ". . . and give Your angels charge over those who sleep."

  Are there others in your household who are preparing for bed or already asleep? Do you have friends or family members who live in other households who are also getting ready for bed? Say their names now as you ask God to watch over and protect them in the night.

  "Tend the sick, we pray . . ."

  Do you know anyone who is sick? Say their names here.

  ". . . give rest to the weary . . ."

  Do you know anyone who is tired either physically or emotionally? Are there people you know who are going through a challenging time in their lives that might have them feeling exhausted? Say their names now as you ask God to give them rest and strength.

". . . soothe the suffering and bless the dying; pity the afflicted . . ."

After this phrase, mention anyone you know who is suffering or facing great challenges of any kind. This phrase is asking God to ease their pain and have compassion on them. This is also the time to mention anyone you know who is near death.

". . . shield the joyous . . ."

Name here anyone you know who is feeling happy and joyful. This is a way of asking God to sustain them in joy.

". . . and all for Your love's sake. Amen."

VARIATIONS

- You can pray this prayer alone as well as with others. You might want to memorize it and say it as a final prayer before falling asleep.
- Research other famous prayers and find a few you like. Some might be morning or midday prayers. You can read these as prayers, memorize and recite them, or use them to guide your praying as in this practice.
- Write your own nighttime prayer. Using your own words, how would you want to pray for friends and family before falling asleep? Share this prayer with the people in your household and invite them to join you in praying the prayer before bed.

Mary Clare says . . .

Often, when we pray, we ask for personal things—to get better from a cold we have, guidance through a rough spot with a friend, or just that we can grow closer to God. This is totally okay, but a large part of praying is also to pray for and bless other people. When my dad and I walked through this practice, we were able to focus on situations and people other than ourselves and our lives, which was really eye-opening.

Many hurricanes had recently hit the South, so we prayed for those who had lost their pets or children, who were hurt or injured, or who were struggling with the hardships that come with destruction. We prayed for those who work, watch, or weep at night, for their healing, and that they would keep hope in their hearts.

Not only did we lift these national concerns up to God, but we were also able to list the names of those that we knew in our community who were sick, tired, or suffering. We prayed for one of my friends, someone from church, and someone in our own family.

This is one of my favorite prayer practices because it includes almost everyone, even those who are joyous—my dad and I were able to pray for their protection. And it was all for the sake of God's love, because God loves all these individuals so much. And I know God is smiling when we take time to pray for others.

Emmaus Walk

On the evening of the day that Jesus was raised from the dead, two disciples, Cleopas and an unnamed companion, were walking from Jerusalem to Emmaus, a seven-mile journey. They were confused about the events of the past few days. They knew that Jesus had been crucified, which devastated them, and they didn't know what to make of recent rumors that he'd been seen alive. They didn't know whether to despair or hope. So, while walking, they engaged in a deep, meaningful conversation about their uncertainty.

As they walked, Jesus himself joined them, but they didn't recognize him. Nonetheless, he joined their conversation all the way to Emmaus. Only when they reached their destination and Jesus stayed with them for a meal did they recognize him as he broke the bread. These disciples had been on a walk, puzzling over something important in their lives, and Jesus had been with them the whole time (Luke 24:13-35).

This prayer practice invites two kids to take a walk together, sharing with each other about a question or puzzle in their lives. Kids do this all the time, of course, on FaceTime, over text, or at school, but this practice gives them the opportunity to do it in a prayerful way, trusting that Jesus through the Spirit is walking with them. It allows them to take their typical conversations and turn them into intentional discernment. Through their sharing and listening, they might be able to hear better God's Spirit speaking through one another and within their own hearts.

This practice will be most appropriate for older kids who possess the capacity for self-reflection and are willing to learn and listen deeply to a friend without judgment or giving advice.

I first experienced this way of prayer on a retreat led by a man named Larry who was my spiritual director at the time. Larry learned the practice from reading a book by Eugene Peterson and Peterson himself learned it from Douglas Steere, a Quaker author and professor.[22] I've never seen written instructions for the practice, so what follows is my own version, written in a way that I hope is useful to kids.

THE PRACTICE

- Before beginning the walk, each of you should spend a few minutes thinking about an issue, challenge, or question in your life that you are dealing with—one you think it might be helpful to talk through with a friend and you would like God's guidance with.
- Get together with a friend in a place where the two of you can take a long, safe walk of about forty minutes. Before you begin walking, stand next to each other for a few moments and imagine God smiling at you. Imagine that God's Spirit is with you already, eager to accompany you on this walk.
- As you walk, take turns sharing. For the first twenty minutes of the walk, one of you will share about the issue, challenge, or question that is on your heart. Maybe this is related to a friendship or another relationship. Maybe it is a question about a decision you have to make, like whether to quit the swim team or audition for the spring play at school. Perhaps you want to share about something that is making you anxious, like the beginning of a new school year. There is no right or wrong thing to share about as long as it is an issue, challenge, or question that is meaningful to you. The most important guideline is to be as honest with yourself and your friend as possible. Sometimes speaking about something out loud while walking can give us new insights and perspectives on a challenge.
- As the first-person shares, the other should listen with an open, curious heart. Your job, as the listener, is to listen deeply to what is being said and to ask occasional questions that might help your friend gain deeper understanding or insight into their situation, or a better sense of how God might be leading them. These might be questions like, "How do you feel about what you are sharing?", "Have you sensed God in this situation, and if so, how?" or "Has

something like this ever happened to you before, and if so, what did you learn from that experience that might be helpful now?" There are a million questions you could ask! Just remember, you want to ask questions that help your friend make more sense of what they are sharing about. If you are listening carefully, trust your instincts to help you ask good questions.

- There is only one rule: You can't give any advice by telling your friend what you think they should do or how they should feel. Only questions! Also, avoid giving advice disguised as a question, like, "Have you ever thought about trying . . . ?"[23] Your job is to ask good questions that can help your friend listen to God and make their own discoveries. The urge to give advice is strong, and it takes some practice to resist the urge and simply ask good, open questions, but once you do—and experience someone doing it for you—you'll know what a gift it is.
- After you have walked for about twenty minutes, and one of you has shared, it's time to switch. As you turn around and head back, the other person gets to share and the first person gets to ask questions, following the same guidelines.
- When you arrive home, get a snack or something to drink, find a place to sit, and have a brief conversation. Talk about how that experience went for each of you. Did either of you sense God's Spirit in any way as you were sharing or listening? Did you gain any new insights or a different perspective on your challenge or question? How did it feel to have someone listening carefully to you without giving advice?
- When you are done, thank your friend for taking this prayerful walk with you and thank God for God's own constant companionship

VARIATIONS

- Do this practice with the same person, once a week, for one month. After four weeks, reflect together about how it's going. Are you getting better at listening? Are you finding the practice feels more natural? Are you sensing God's presence differently?
- Do this practice with a parent or grown-up you trust, then spend some time thinking about how that felt. Was it nice to have a grown-up listen to you without giving advice? Did it feel weird for a grown-up to share with you about something going on in their life as you listened and asked questions?
- Do this practice as a group. Take a walk in pairs, and when everyone returns, get a snack and talk together about how it went. This could be a good activity for a youth group or a Sunday school class.

chapter eighteen
Ways to Pray for Justice

Housing

When our family is driving around Pittsburgh, it's not uncommon to see someone standing on a street corner with a sign that reads, "Homeless—Anything Helps." They might pace along the sidewalk, carrying their sign past the cars lined up at a stoplight. When this happens, we frantically rifle through the car for something we can give—an apple, a bottle of water, a granola bar. Occasionally, we'll give the person a couple of dollars.

A church we were part of once invited kids and youth to make care bags for people experiencing homelessness. The kids researched what would be the most useful for those living in tents or shelters, under bridges, or in their cars. Then, after shopping for the items, they gathered at the church and assembled the items, putting them in one-gallon freezer bags. Mary Clare brought home several of these bags, and we kept them in our car so that we would have something to give to people asking for help. Whenever we handed someone a bag, we shared our names and asked them for theirs. If time permitted, we would engage in longer conversation.

The bags the kids made that day—and the ones we have made since—typically include a granola bar or an energy bar, a bottle of water, a bag of chips, sunscreen, and a couple pairs of new socks.

Wherever Jesus went, he made it a habit to pause and show tangible compassion to people asking for help. At one point, he told his disciples to "give to anyone who begs from you," and another time he told them that whenever they give food or water to someone in need, they are giving it to him (see Luke 6:30 and Matt. 25:40). Creating these care bags and using the prayer guide below can help grown-ups and kids embody the compassion of Jesus. It can also help them become more aware of housing issues in their local communities, inspiring their imaginations about other ways they and their congregations can practice Christ-like compassion.

THE PRACTICE

- With the help of a grown-up, research homelessness in your community. Try to find out who is most likely to be—or become—unhoused and why. See if you can discover what people in your area are already doing to address the situation of people lacking shelter. Are there shelters in your community where the unhoused can sleep? Are there agencies that are working with people experiencing homelessness to help them find a safe place to live? Share what you are learning with someone you know.
- As part of your research, explore what kinds of items would be helpful in a care bag, like energy bars, socks, water, a box of raisins, bags of trail mix, and sunscreen. You could have a grown-up help you call a shelter and ask someone who works there.
- After you've decided what you want to put in the bags, get a grown-up to take you shopping and purchase what you need along with one-gallon freezer bags to hold the items. Think about inviting

some friends to go with you. When you get home, assemble the bags, placing one of each item you bought in a plastic bag.

- Once the bags are assembled, hold one in your hand and imagine God smiling at you. God is finding joy in your concern for people who are struggling to find good, safe housing.
- Now as you hold the bag, imagine the person who might receive this bag. It could be someone you have seen before on a street corner. Are you imagining a single person or a few different people? Do they have children? Maybe a dog? Where do you see them—on a street corner or at a bus stop? Try to imagine what their challenges might be throughout the day—finding transportation, buying food, finding a place to shower, getting good rest, or simply feeling safe.
- Imagine God smiling on them—God loves them so much. But God is also sad that they are experiencing these struggles. Imagine God's love, peace, and protection falling on them like rain. Continue to imagine this in silence for a few moments.
- Then place your hand on top of the bag and say the following prayer or one like it:

> *God of compassion, bless this bag and whoever receives it. May the items in this bag be helpful to them and make their life a little bit easier. May they know how much you love them and never doubt that you are on their side. May giving this bag away be a part of your own love and compassion at work in the world. Amen.*

- Make sure to store a couple of these bags in the car you ride in with the grown-ups in your life. Offer one to anyone in need when the opportunity arises. As you are riding away after you hand someone a bag, whisper a prayer asking God to bless them and send others their way who can help them find a safe place to live.

VARIATIONS

- Get a youth group or Sunday school class to do this activity together. A couple of weeks after putting the bags together, have a conversation about what giving them away has been like: What did you notice, experience, or learn in the process? Where did you sense God's presence along the way?
- Do some more research on ways to address issues related to housing and homelessness. Ask a pastor what your church is doing to help people who are unhoused.
- Get a grown-up to take you to visit a shelter for people who are unhoused. Have the grown-up call ahead to find out if visiting would be okay. While you are there to learn as much as you can about what they do and how they run their organization, check to see if there are any opportunities for volunteering. Share with your Sunday school class, youth group, or family what you learned and take time to pray for the people staying in the shelter.

Mary Clare says . . .

Often, when we drive through the city, we'll see someone on a corner or the sidewalk with their belongings in a bag and holding a cardboard sign that says something like, "Homeless and hungry, anything helps. God bless." It breaks my heart every time when we don't have something to give them. Once when we drove past someone with a sign, I remembered the bags we used to make and give out and asked parents if we could make more.

Shortly after, my mom and I stopped by a local Walmart with a list of things that we could add to these bags—energy bars, bottled water, face wipes, dry shampoo, socks, chapstick, toothbrushes, toothpaste—anything that someone could use in their everyday life. We even bought some lollipops as a little treat.

At home, Mom, Dad, and I sat in a circle and set up an assembly line of sorts. The three of us were assigned a group of items and would place one in each drawstring bag before passing it to the next person to add their items. Before long, we had ten bags full of non-perishable food, hygiene items, and warm socks that were ready to be blessed and handed out.

My dad read the first half of the blessing from this prayer practice then got choked-up (so on-brand for him!) so I read the second half. We placed our hands on one of the bags and focused our attention on imagining the person who would receive this bag. Taking time to pray for their wellbeing, wherever they may be, and asking that this bag may help them is a meaningful part of the process.

It's important to realize that the people on the side of the road are humans too, with emotions, needs, and wants. And, most of all, that God loves and values them so much. Every time we can hand one of these bags out, we are taking part in God's kingdom and sharing God's everlasting love.

Food Insecurity

It was at the end of a long day of teaching, and thousands of people had been gathered to listen to what Jesus had to say. By now, no doubt, they were hungry. The disciples suggested that Jesus dismiss them so that they could go into town and buy dinner, but Jesus replied, "*You* give them something to eat." The disciples were shocked—how could they feed all these people? The Gospel of John says a small boy in the crowd was willing to share what he had. And that was all Jesus needed—some bread and a few fish—to feed several thousand people (Mark 6:30-44; John 6:1-14).

When we think about this story, we often focus on the miracle of Jesus multiplying a small amount of food into a whole lot, but we forget that someone first shared what they had, not knowing what would happen next. And that this person was a kid.

We live in world that has plenty of food—much of which is ultimately thrown in the trash—and still many people in our communities experience food insecurity. They either don't have enough food to feed themselves and their families, or they are on the brink of not having enough. Many people live in places where healthy, whole food is either scarce or too expensive.

It's unlikely that a few kids are going to rectify this unjust situation—it is complex and systemic—but the miracle of the feeding of the 5,000 shows that what little they can do matters. This prayer practice gives kids the opportunity to *do* something—to learn about food insecurity in their communities, to collect food for those in need, and to pray both for people who are struggling with food insecurity and the organizations working to ensure everyone has enough to eat.

This practice invites kids to remember that it breaks God's heart whenever anyone goes to bed hungry, especially kids.

THE PRACTICE

- With the help of a grown-up, do some research on hunger and food insecurity where you live. What does food insecurity mean? How many people experience food insecurity? What are some of the causes of food insecurity? What organizations and agencies in your community are trying to help? Where in your area is food being collected and given to people who need it? What else are people doing to address this problem?
- Get a grown-up to help you check with a local food bank to find out what kinds of food they need most. Then go shopping for

those items or look in your kitchen cabinets to see if you have any food you can donate to the food bank. You might want to invite some friends to join you in this.

- Once you have gathered the food you are going to donate, place the items on a table or on the floor in front of you and take some time to pray. For a few moments, imagine God smiling at you. Imagine how glad God feels to know there are kids like you who want to help those who don't have enough food. Imagine that God is smiling on them too, because God loves them so much and it breaks God's heart that they are hungry in a world where there is so much food.
- In silence, imagine the people who might receive this food. Some of them are likely seniors, while others are much younger. How do you think these people are feeling—sad that they don't have as much food as they need? Thankful for the generosity of people who help? Confused about why their struggles exist in a world with so much food?
- Imagine God's love and compassion flowing into them. Try to feel how much God loves them and how sad God is about their situation. Think about how God wants them to have enough food to live healthy, happy lives. Simply be still for a few moments as you imagine God's love flowing into the people who will receive this food.
- Place your hand on the food—if others are with you, they can do this too—and pray this prayer or one like it:

> *God of compassion, bless this food and those who will receive it. May it give strength and nourishment to their bodies, and may this food be a sign for them of your love and compassion. Bless all those who work to end the injustice of food insecurity. Thank you for their service and give them the strength to carry*

on. May we live in a world where everyone is willing to share, trusting that there is enough for all. Amen.

- After you have prayed, have an adult help you deliver the food to a local food bank where it will be distributed to those in need. While you are there, learn more about what they do and any opportunities to volunteer.

VARIATIONS

- Continue to do this monthly, making it a priority in your home. If you can, whenever you shop for food (or a grown-up in your house does) purchase one item to be given away. At the end of each month, take the food you have collected to a food bank.
- Talk to a classroom teacher at your school, your Sunday school teacher, or youth minister about collecting food as a group. Decorate a box to put in your classroom or at your church for the food to be collected in.
- As you pray with your family at meals, remember to pray for those who don't have enough food. Then have a conversation with the people you live with about how you can make a difference.

Climate Justice

As I am writing this, the strongest hurricane to ever form in the Atlantic this early in hurricane season is wreaking havoc in the Caribbean. Additionally, over one hundred million people are under high temperature warnings in the United States. Wildfires are ravaging Arizona and California, and Iowans are recovering from devastating floods. While these kinds of severe weather events happen every year, they are becoming stronger and more frequent because of climate change. They indicate the deterioration of the world that God called human beings to steward well.

Though no one is immune from these effects, they are experienced disproportionately by people in poverty and by those living in poorer, less developed countries. Climate change is an issue of justice.

This prayer practice affords kids the opportunity to understand the effects of climate change, consider how they can work to protect our world and vulnerable populations, and allow the challenge of climate change to become part of their life of prayer.

A word of caution: Introducing kids to overwhelming challenges like climate change, over which we have little direct control, can elicit fear and anxiety. Child and adolescent psychologists are already reporting anxiety in young people caused by fears related to the changing climate. Older kids are likely aware of climate change but perhaps have not thought of the injustices associated with it, as people in poorer countries suffer the most. This prayer practice should take place with adult guidance and be adapted so that it is age appropriate. Grown-ups using this with children should be attentive to how the kids are responding and make appropriate adjustments. They should be available for conversation with kids to reassure them and create a sense of safety.

THE PRACTICE

- With the help of a grown-up, do some research on climate change and climate justice. Search for answers to questions like: What do scientists think are the causes of climate change? What are the effects of climate change, especially in the region where you live? Who around the world is most likely to experience the negative effects of climate change and why? What are people doing to slow climate change and protect those who are most vulnerable? If doing this research causes any fear or anxiety in you, stop and talk to a grown-up you trust about how you are feeling.

- After you have learned about climate change, find a comfortable place to pray and spend a few moments thinking about how God is smiling at you and how glad God is that you care so much for this world that God loves—along with all the people and animals in it. Take a few moments to thank God silently for the gift of this this beautiful earth.
- Now recall some of the research you have done about climate change, especially about the people who will suffer the most as the planet continues to warm. This problem can feel too big! It can feel overwhelming and scary! Hold your palms open in your lap and imagine that you are holding this challenge of climate change in your hands. Then lift your hands as if you are handing all of this to God. As you do, silently pray something like, "God, this problem feels so big I hardly know what to do, but I hold it up to you, knowing that you are holding it too and that I can't fix it by myself. I hold before you in prayer this world that you love and the people, plants, and animals in it. I also give to you my own fears and worries."
- As you lower your hands into your lap, allow yourself to feel the peace that comes from releasing worries to God.
- Spend some time thinking about the ways you learned that people are making a difference to slow climate change, protect God's world, and help those who suffer most from climate change. Did anything you learned inspire you? Is there something—a small thing—you can do, even if right now that is only learning more and having conversations with others about climate change? Say to God, "God help me to care more deeply about this world and all the plants, animals, and people you love so much. I feel so small but help me to know if there is something I can do to make a difference."

- Spend some time in silence, paying attention to what is in your heart. Are you imagining any ways you can be a part of protecting God's world?
- When you are finished, spend a few more moments resting in God's presence. Thank God for always being with you and for God's love for every creature. Allow yourself to feel safe and secure in God's loving embrace.

VARIATIONS

- Get some friends to do this practice together. After you have researched and prayed, talk together about what you can do. Are there people in your community who are already advocating for climate justice that you can join with or support?
- After you have done some research, get a world map and circle the places where people will be most affected by climate change. As part of your prayer time, pray for the people in these places, saying, "God, I lift up to you the people of ________," "I lift up to you the people of ________," and so on.
- Talk to leaders in your church or your children's or youth minister about what your church is doing to respond to climate justice and to care for creation. Tell them that this matters to you and ask them if you can help get something started.

Bad News

Kids know more about what's going on in the world, both nearby and far away, than we give them credit for. They see the headlines, overhear what adults are listening to on the radio and podcasts, and gather snippets of information from the conversations going on around them. We often try to shield kids from bad news, like stories about racial injustice, war, gun violence, and other crises. But they know these things are going on. After all, these kids are already accustomed to learning to "run, hide, fight" if a violent intruder breaks into their school. They are often more aware than we would like them to be.

Why not equip them to bring the bad news they already know about into their relationship with God? When we feel helpless in the face of a crisis or situation of injustice, spending time in prayer about it can feel productive; it can ease anxiety and fear. Prayer can also inspire us and the kids we are working with to take appropriate action to address the challenges we hear about in the news.

This prayer practice will require significant adult guidance, depending on the age of the kids involved. Care needs to be taken selecting a news story to pray about so that kids won't become overwhelmed by bad news and feel helpless and afraid.

The following outline of the prayer practice can be adapted to use with kids to pray about any difficult or challenging situation they learn about.

THE PRACTICE

- With the help of a grown-up, find a story in the news that deals with a challenge, crisis, or difficult situation in your community, your country, or the world. This story can be about any number of things—racism, poverty, antisemitism, war, political division, or any of the many ways hatred shows up in our world. Make sure your grown-up helps you find an article that is appropriate for a kid your age and won't make you too anxious or afraid.
- Before talking about the news story with your grown-up, spend a few moments together imagining that God is smiling on you. God loves you so much and wants you to be safe and feel safe. Thank God for being with you and ask God to give you a sense of peace as you discuss a news story about a difficult situation.

- Take some time to discuss the news story with the grown-up you are with. Ask questions that help you understand what is going on in the story. Be sure to talk about how this story is making you feel, whether nervous or afraid, confused or overwhelmed. In the presence of God and with this grown-up who loves you, remember that you are safe and secure.
- After spending some time talking about this news story, take time to pray out loud for the situation addressed in the story. Pray for whatever comes to mind. You and your grown-up can take turns praying, trading back and forth, until you sense that you have said to God everything that is on your heart. You can pray:
  - For the people who are involved in this situation, that they would be safe and secure.
  - That God's presence and peace would be felt in the situation, whatever it is.
  - By sharing with God your own feelings related to this situation, whether you are feeling peace or a sense of worry.
  - That God would help you imagine something you can do to make the situation better and show God's love.
- After praying out loud, take a few moments to hold your hands open in your lap, and then lift them silently to God, as if you are lifting this news story and all the people in it up to God, acknowledging that it is too big for you to deal with on your own. God is with you, lovingly carrying the burden of this bad news.
- After a few moments of holding your hands up to God in this way, say, "Amen."
- End by talking to the grown-up you are praying with about how this experience of prayer and conversation was for you and how you are feeling now. Share anything that came to mind that you can do to show love and compassion to the people in the situation in the news story.

VARIATIONS

- Under the guidance of an adult, do this prayer practice with a Sunday school class or a youth group, having a wider conversation about what's going on in the world and then bringing it before God in prayer.
- Do this practice once a week either with the same news story or with related news stories. At the end of one month, have a conversation about how you are feeling now, and notice what has changed in you or the situation you have been praying about over the course of a month.
- Use this prayer practice to pray for any challenging situation, even if it's not in the news. Is there a difficult situation in your school or among your friends that this guide could help you pray about?

a final word

The other day I picked up Mary Clare at the end of the first full day marching band camp. She is no longer the young girl I wrote about in the introduction to this book nor the thirteen-year-old she was when we started working on *Praying Their Way* together. She is fifteen and quickly approaching the start of her sophomore year in high school.

When she got in the car, lugging a backpack and a saxophone case, she told me she was tired and had a headache. They'd marched outside in the ninety-degree heat, and the air conditioning wasn't working in the building—it was eighty degrees in the band room. Her back and hips hurt, and she was exhausted. A bunch of her friends were going to hang out that evening, but she was too tired; she didn't want to go.

"All day," she said, "I've been repeating 'save us from the time of trial.' That's been my prayer phrase today—because there have been a lot of trials!"[24]

I heard beneath her litany of complaints nostalgia for a younger age, so recent in her memory, when summer vacations meant lounging at the pool every day with a few friends, hoping their parents would let them buy lunch at the snack bar—not taking an online health class and reviewing French and two weeks of band camp and daily tennis clinics to get prepared for tryouts. Nostalgia for summers with fewer trials.

As she spoke, I remembered how less than a week earlier I'd asked her about her goals for the new school years. She told me that one of her goals was to publish a poem, even if only in the school literary magazine. Another was to, as she put it, "do a better job of remembering God throughout the day." She said, "I realize I just go through the day and hardly think about God. Does that happen to you?"

"Of course it does," I told her.

I thought of that conversation while we were driving home from band camp, because I saw in her repeating a phrase of the Lord's Prayer throughout the day an attempt to live into her desire to remember God. *Good for her*, I thought.

I also realized, with gladness burgeoning in my heart, that this is *exactly* what I had hoped our book, *Praying Their Way*, would help make possible: kids, noticing their own longing for God; kids, acting on that longing; kids, finding their way into friendship with God. Kids, not letting headache-inducing heat stand in the way of prayer.

And kids and adults together sharing the journey. Chatting about life with God in the car like you would what's for dinner and whether, after dinner, you should go to Jerry's for frozen custard or Emmerling's for ice cream.

Conversation about God and prayer, as natural as anything else.

Here is my hope: that this book is becoming dog-eared and underlined, that the pages are getting worn. That the words in this book get translated again and again to speak to the conditions of your life and the needs of the kids in your life. That, like a favorite old shoe, the shape of the book changes to fit the contour your life with kids, whether that's a family, a church, or a group of friends. That you are making it your own. Books about prayer are nothing if they don't become used and useful.

I also hope that you find the book worth sharing with others: friends, relatives, ministers. Don't let your own growth in friendship with

God—and the growth that you are seeing in the kids in your life—stay private. Tell someone else and share this book if it's been helpful.

But most of all, I hope that this book is fostering connection—connection between grown-ups and kids as the sometimes-challenging subject of prayer becomes less intimidating to talk about, and adults and kids both grow more confident in discussing prayer. And in *praying*.

And, most importantly, connection between kids and God—the God who is simply bursting with delight in them.

Picture it—can you?—that smile on God's face.

notes

1. The song is a Taizé chant called "Nothing Can Trouble" and can be found in *Songs & Prayers from Taizé* (Chicago: GIA Publications, Inc., 1991), 29.
2. This is a paraphrase of the way Anthony de Mello. S.J., tells the story in his *The Song of the Bird* (New York: Image Books, 1982), 12-13.
3. This is my very loose translation/paraphrase of what Augustine says in his *Confessions*. Henry Chadwick translates the phrase more literally: "But you were more inward than my most inward part . . ." St. Augustine, *Confessions*, trans. Henry Chadwick (Oxford: Oxford University Press, 1991), 43.
4. Martin Laird, O.S.A., *Into the Silent Land* (New York: Oxford University Press, 2006), 15.
5. See chapter 49 of *Revelations of Divine Love*, in which Julian of Norwich writes, "No anger is found in God." Julian of Norwich, *Revelations of Divine Love*, trans. Clifton Wolters (London: Penguin Books, 1966), 139.
6. Thomas R. Kelly, *A Testament of Devotion* (New York: HarperCollins, 1969), 6.
7. John Mogabgab, "Editor's Introduction," *Weavings*, July/August 1992, 2.
8. When I was young, I had a pastor who, in a whispery voice, would go on and on when he prayed. His favorite word, which he used repeatedly, was "unstoppable." That seemed appropriate to me because the word described his prayers: I thought they would never stop!
9. This is the very advice James Clear offers to help establish any new habit. See his *Atomic Habits* (New York: Avery, 2018), 71.
10. I borrow this analogy from Marjorie Thompson, *Soul Feast*, Newly Revised Edition, (Louisville, KY: Westminster John Knox, 2014), 17.

11. Martin Luther, "Preface to the Psalter," trans. Charles M. Jacobs, in *Luther's Works*, vol. 35: *Word and Sacrament*, ed. E. Theodore Bachman (Philadelphia: Muhlenberg Press, 1960), 254.
12. John Cassian, *Conferences*, The Classics of Western Spirituality, trans. Colm Luibheid (New York: Paulist Press, 1985), 132-134.
13. See chapter 3, "The Quiet Center," in L. Roger Owens, *What We Need Is Here: Practicing the Heart of Christian Spirituality* (Nashville: Upper Room Books, 2015), 53-67.
14. Elise S. Eslinger, ed., *Upper Room Worshipbook* (Nashville: Upper Room Books, 2006), 8.
15. Thompson, *Soul Feast*, 41.
16. Julian of Norwich, *Revelations*, 169.
17. See Paul Tillich, *The Courage to Be*, second edition (New Haven: Yale University Press, 2000), 156, 185-190.
18. *Early Christian Writings: The Apostolic Fathers*, trans. Maxwell Stamforth; rev. trans. Andrew Louth (London: Penguin Books, 1968; 1987), 194.
19. Along with listening to God in nature, Thompson lists several other ways we can listen to God including through others, the circumstances of our lives, and our own intuition. See Thompson, *Soul Feast*, 33-36.
20. Philip Jacob Spener, *Pia Diesideria*, trans. and ed. Theodore G. Tappert (Fortress Press, 1964), 89-95.
21. Robert Benson, *Venite: A Book of Daily Prayer* (New York: Tarcher/Putnam, 2000), 15.
22. Eugene H. Peterson, *The Pastor: A Memoir* (New York: HarperOne, 2011), 218-22.
23. On not giving advise disguised as a question, see Parker Palmer, *A Hidden Wholeness: The Journey Toward an Undivided Life* (San Francisco: Jossey-Bass, 2004), 132-134.
24. "Save us from the time of trial" is the way the Ecumenical Version of the Lord's Prayer expresses the more traditional phrase "lead us not into temptation."

acknowledgments

We are deeply grateful to the team at Upper Room Books for shepherding *Praying Their Way* from concept to reality, especially: Michael Stephens, for believing in this book from the start; Benjamin Howard, for his careful editing and care with words; and Deborah Arca, for her dedication to helping this book find an audience (and for having the great idea for a backpack on the cover!). We appreciate the hospitality of the baristas at Starbucks in Harmer, PA, where the two of us spent many hours with our laptops open in front of us, sipping lattes and writing.

Roger is grateful for the support and encouragement of his colleagues at Pittsburgh Theological Seminary and for the gift of being able to teach at an institution that values their faculty writing books for the church as well as the academy.

Finally, we dedicate this book to Ginger (aka, Mom) for reasons too many to list. Let us just say: Thank you for your love, nurture, and support—we love you!

For those who hunger for deep spiritual experience . . .

The Academy for Spiritual Formation® is an experience of disciplined Christian community emphasizing holistic spirituality—nurturing body, mind, and spirit. The program, a ministry of The Upper Room®, is ecumenical in nature and meant for all those who hunger for a deeper relationship with God, including both lay and clergy persons. Each Academy fosters spiritual rhythms—of study and prayer, silence and liturgy, solitude and relationship, rest and play.

With offerings of both Two-Year and Five-Day models, Academy participants rediscover Christianity's rich spiritual heritage through worship, learning, and fellowship. During the Two-Year Academy, pilgrims gather at a retreat center for five days every three months over the course of two years (a total of 40 days), and the Five-Day Academy is a modified version of the Two-Year experience, inviting pilgrims to gather for five days of spiritual learning and worship. The Academy's commitment to an authentic spirituality promotes balance, inner and outer peace, holy living and justice living—God's shalom.

Faculty trained in the wide breadth of Christian spirituality and practice provide content and guidance at each session of The Academy. Academy faculty presenters come from seminaries, monasteries, spiritual direction ministries, and pastoral ministries or other settings and are from a variety of traditions.

The Academy Recommends program seeks to highlight content that aligns with the Academy's mission to create transformative space for people to connect with God, self, others, and creation for the sake of the world.

Learn more by visiting academy.upperroom.org.